William C. Stewart

The practical Angler

Or The Art of Trout-fishing, more particularly applied to Clear Water

William C. Stewart

The practical Angler
Or The Art of Trout-fishing, more particularly applied to Clear Water

ISBN/EAN: 9783337141424

Printed in Europe, USA, Canada, Australia, Japan

Cover: Foto ©Lupo / pixelio.de

More available books at **www.hansebooks.com**

THE

PRACTICAL ANGLER

OR

THE ART OF TROUT-FISHING

MORE PARTICULARLY APPLIED TO CLEAR WATER

BY W. C. STEWART

FIFTH EDITION REVISED AND ENLARGED

EDINBURGH

ADAM AND CHARLES BLACK

1867

PRINTED BY R. CLARK, EDINBURGH.

PREFACE.

—◆—

MOST anglers meet with fair success when the waters are dark coloured; but when the waters are clear they find poor sport. This is mainly due to an erroneous system of fishing, which angling works already published have done little to remove, and which, though its effects were not so observable fifty years ago, when drainage was less extensively in operation, and when the streams continued large and discoloured for some time, is not at all adapted for the small clear waters of the present day. It is with the view of showing how almost, if not quite, as good sport may be had in clear water as in coloured, that we have undertaken to add another to the numerous volumes already existing upon this very popular amusement. It is almost unnecessary to add, that as it is more difficult to deceive trout in clear water than in coloured, the method of angling which succeeds best in the one case will also succeed best in the other.

For more than fifteen years we have pursued angling with the greatest assiduity ; and during that period have obtained information from a number of excellent amateur anglers (among whom we may mention the Secretary of the late St. Ronan's Angling Club), to all of whom we take this opportunity of expressing our thanks. We have also fished with, and watched while fishing, almost all the best professional anglers of the day, including the celebrated James Baillie, considered by all who know him the ablest fly-fisher in Scotland, and from whom we have received some valuable information upon that branch of the art ; and it must be admitted that there are few anglers like those whose ingenuity and perseverance are stimulated by necessity. The information received from these we have thoroughly tested before admitting it into the following pages; and we may safely say that we have gained more from half an hour's conversation with such, than from all the books we ever read upon the subject, and their number is not small; most works upon angling being rather amusing than instructive. The angler will not find this the case in the following volume; if he finds nothing instructive, he will certainly find nothing amusing; and we found our claims to the attention of the angling community solely upon the ground of the information we have to convey, which we have endeavoured to make as distinct as possible; and as this treatise is only intended for anglers, we expect that the style and composition will not be very severely criticised.

EDINBURGH, *January* 1857.

PREFACE TO THE FOURTH EDITION.

HE reception which the *Practical Angler* met with when first published, four years ago, was highly gratifying. The press, as our readers will see by the appendix to this volume, expressed a very favourable opinion; and since then it has gone through three editions—an amount of success which shows clearly that what the angling community now want, is not another amusing description of the pleasures of angling, but a book to teach them how to fish.

In other respects, also, the success of the *Practical Angler* has been quite up to our expectations, not that it has made a first-rate angler of every one who has read its pages ; very far from this. It is one thing to be told how to

fish, it is another and much more difficult thing
to do it successfully ; but the theory of angling
therein explained has been generally received
as correct, and if the angler cannot put it in
practice it is his own fault. Most of our
readers, however, admit having derived some
benefit from these pages, and we have received
numerous letters from anglers residing in all
parts of the kingdom mentioning this, and
stating that their baskets now present a very
different appearance on their return from a day's
angling. It is, however, painful to be compelled
to admit that there is a very large number of
anglers who have never read this volume at all,
giving as a reason that they know all that is in
it already and can fish well enough. Now, if
these were first-rate anglers there would be some
excuse for them, but they are by no means so,
and it would be difficult to understand the state
of their minds, but that *Blackwood's Magazine*
has most opportunely solved the problem. The
reviewer of this volume in that periodical says—
" that darkness rather than light is the deliberate
choice of the million. The best teaching in the

world is thrown away upon stupidity and self-conceit, and that not only in ethics, but in such practical matters as angling."

There can be no doubt that the reviewer has here hit upon the two causes of all the ignorance that is in the world, and we, as may be expected, are quite willing to lay the flattering unction to our souls, and to ascribe to these causes the ignorance of those who know no more about fishing than they did before the *Practical Angler* was published.

The most unpleasant part of our duty remains to be done, and that is to apologise to a very large number of correspondents whose communications we have been unable to answer. In the first edition, in a moment of heedless enthusiasm, we promised to send pattern flies to any one who wished to see them. We had not the most remote idea of the labour this would entail upon us; hundreds of letters poured in, and gross after gross of flies went the way whence they did not return ; and after sending away all the flies which we had intended to serve us for years, no resource remained but to call a halt and leave the communications unanswered, as we had neither the flies to send nor the time to write; and we hope this explanation will satisfy our correspondents.

In laying before the public this edition of the *Practical Angler* we have revised it carefully and embodied in it any additional information obtained during the last four years. We have also endeavoured to make some passages which correspondents complained of, easier of comprehension. In the preface to the first edition, we stated that our object in publishing was to show how almost, if not quite, as good sport may be had in clear water as in coloured. Subsequent experience has convinced us that not only as good, but better sport may be had in clear water than in coloured. Why it is so will be explained in this volume ; and, in conclusion, we have only to hope that those anglers who have benefited from a perusal of the first edition, will find their education completed by a careful study of the fourth.

CONTENTS.

CHAPTER I.

INTRODUCTORY.

CHAPTER II.

FRESH-WATER TROUT.

CHAPTER III.

ANGLER'S ' EQUIPMENT.

CHAPTER VII.

ON ANGLING WITH THE WORM.

CHAPTER VIII.

MAY-FLY FISHING.

CHAPTER IX.

MINNOW AND PARR-TAIL FISHING.

CHAPTER X.

LOCH-FISHING.

CHAPTER XI.

APPLICATION.

PRACTICAL ANGLER.

CHAPTER I.

INTRODUCTORY.

NGLERS, unlike excisemen, have no ground of complaint against the definition given of their occupation in Johnson's Dictionary. Angling, the world is there informed, is "the art of fishing with a rod." This may be imperfect—may need a little filling up (the task, indeed, which we propose to ourselves)—but it is perfectly fair and unprejudiced. Not so, however, another definition, dropped from the lips of the same great authority in private, and which has ever since passed from mouth to mouth with a sneer. "Angling," said Dr. Johnson, "means a rod with a fly at one end and a fool at the other." Nothing has rankled so deeply in the angling mind as this *obiter dictum* of the Mitre. It came from one, however, who knew nothing whatever about the pursuit at which he threw his sarcasm, who, short-sighted and hypochondriacal, probably

could not have enjoyed it had he tried, and who
(the fact is sufficient for us) openly proclaimed his
preference for the tumult of Fleet Street to the
finest rural scene in England. Still, we are bound
to confess, that the British public is to a considerable
extent divided as to which definition is the more
correct. There are few amusements which the uninitiated look upon as so utterly stupid ; and an
angler seems generally regarded as at best a simple-
ton, whose only merit, if he succeeds, is that of unlimited patience, and whose want of success—should
he not succeed—is only attributable to his want of
that virtue, of which people seem to take fully more
credit for the want than for the possession. Such
impressions can only have originated in very confused
ideas of both angling and patience ; and though it
may suit the unsuccessful to abuse angling as
" slow" and monotonous, and to quote Dr. Johnson's
famous saying—which, so far as they are concerned,
is certainly correct—angling, as we hope to show, is
by no means either slow or simple, and requires just
the same qualifications as are required for success in
any other pursuit—viz. energy and skill, and those
in no small degree.

If, however, on the one hand angling is looked
upon with little favour by an unenlightened multi-
tude, on the other hand there is no amusement to
which those who practise it become so much attached.
Nor do we think that anglers generally can fairly be
accused either of stupidity, or, let us say, patience.

They have certainly in their ranks a larger proportion of men of literature and science than can
be found among the followers of any other field
sport; and for the comfort of those who have not the
much-despised gift of patience, we could point to a
number of celebrated anglers, who are by no means
celebrated as possessing this virtue, while numbers
of the most patient followers of Izaak Walton are
very far from having rivalled his success.   Angling,
when once embarked in by any person possessed of a
reasonable amount of soul and brains, becomes a pas-
sion, and like other passions will grow and feed upon
the smallest possible amount of encouragement. Fish
or no fish, whenever opportunity offers, the angler
may be found at the water-side. If this only went on
in fine weather, people could understand it, but now-
a-days, even in summer, the weather is not always
fine; and when a man is seen standing in the water
for hours in a torrent of rain, with benumbed hands
and an empty basket, doubts of the individual's
sanity naturally suggest themselves, mixed with
feelings of pity for the terrible consequences in the
way of colds, rheumatism, etc., which it is supposed
must inevitably follow, but which don't. We have
it from high medical authority, that rheumatism is
more engendered by hot rooms and fires than by
exposure, and as for the comfort of the thing, that
is according to taste. It is surely better to have fresh
air and exercise, even in wet, than to be spending
the whole day in some country inn, yawning over

some second-rate novel for the third time, the amusement agreeably diversified by staring out of the window at the interminable rain, by poking a peat-fire, and possibly by indulging in a superfluity of that institution of the country, pale ale.

> " Though sluggards deem it but an idle chase,
> And marvel men should quit their easy chair
> The toilsome way and long long league to trace ;
> Oh ! there is sweetness in the mountain air,
> And life that bloated ease can never hope to share."

That angling is good for exercise is certain. That it is also good for amusement is equally certain ; but the pleasure derived from the catching of fish, like that derived from other field sports, is more easily felt than described. There can be no doubt, that by the great majority of people an amusement is valued in proportion as it affords room for the exercise of skill—there is more merit, and therefore more pleasure in excelling in what is difficult—and though we may astonish some of our readers, we assert, and shall endeavour to prove, that angling is the most difficult of all field sports. It requires all the manual dexterity that the others do, and brings more into play the qualities of the mind, observation, and the reasoning faculties. In shooting and hunting, the dogs do the observation and the reasoning part of the business, and the sportsman the mechanical ; but the angler has not only to find out where his fish are, but to catch them, and that not by such a " knock-me-down" method as is practised upon some unfortunate blackcock or unwary hare, but by an art of deception. The angler's wits, in fact, are brought into direct competition with those of the fish, which very often, judging from the result, prove the better of the two.

Besides the mere pleasure of fishing, however, angling has more varied attractions than almost any other amusement. To the lover of nature no sport affords so much pleasure. The grandest and most picturesque scenes in nature are to be found on the banks of rivers and lakes. The angler, therefore, enjoys the finest scenery the country offers; and, whereas other sportsmen are limited to particular places and seasons, he can follow his vocation alike on lowland stream or highland loch, and during the whole six months in which the country is most inviting. From April, with her budding trees and singing birds, to May and June, with their meadows decked with the daisy and the primrose, and breezes scented with the hawthorn and wild thyme, and on to autumn, with her " fields white unto the harvest," he sees all that is beautiful—all that is exhilarating—all that is grand and elevating in this world of ours, which, whatever people may say, is not such a bad world after all, if they would only keep bleach-fields and blackguards off the rivers' banks.

With this brief resumé of some of the principal attractions of angling we must content ourselves. We have neither space, inclination, nor ability, to do justice to this branch of the subject. Furthermore, it is unnecessary, as the ground in this respect is already fully occupied ; and if any one wishes to have all the joys of angling set forth in genuine old English style, let him read Izaak Walton, " being a discourse on fish and fishing not unworthy the perusal of most anglers." Here may be found a conglomeration of fertile meadows, crystal brooks, meandering streams, milk-maids' songs, and moral reflections, which must prove irresistible ; and also, if a man of tender conscience, be able to satisfy himself that angling is not a cruel amusement, though it must be admitted that some of Izaak's injunctions, such as putting a hook " through a frog tenderly, as though you loved him,"—seeing that the said tenderness is to be evinced, not for the sake of saving the frog's feelings, but of prolonging its wretched life— do savour a little of harshness, and seem to justify Lord Byron's lines :—

" The quaint old cruel coxcomb in his gullet
  Should have a hook, and a small trout to pull it."

Never having had any scruples of this sort ourselves, we have not studied the subject, and therefore leave the defence of it to Walton and a celebrated Doctor of Divinity who has taken it in hand ; but if any one has any scruples, or thinks angling slow and stupid, or has any other objections, let him keep clear of it by all means. There are plenty of anglers already, and every year adds to the list a number, who are not to be deterred either by the sneers of this world, or by terror of the punishment, which, the poet thinks, should be reserved for the master, and we suppose for all his followers, in the next ; and our purpose is not to make more anglers, but to make successful anglers of those unsuccessful at present.

Some fish afford more sport in their capture than others ; but for whatever kind necessity may compel the angler to fish, its capture will always afford him amusement, provided he has not been accustomed to anything superior. The juvenile cockney who bobs for gudgeon and eels in the dubs and ditches in the neighbourhood of London, and whom a trout of a pound weight would scare out of a year's growth, plies his lure as unremittingly as the sportsman who captures the monarch of the streams in some noble river, such as Tweed or Tay.

Of all the inhabitants of the fresh water, no fish is looked upon with such favour by the angler, and none affords him such varied and continuous sport, as the common fresh-water trout. This is owing to its being the most difficult to capture of all the finny tribe, not excepting the salmon itself, to the sport it affords when hooked—the trout being stronger than any fish of its size—and to its fine edible qualities.

In some parts of England trout have almost disappeared, and the angler has been compelled to have recourse to meaner fare ; but in Scotland trout are more plentiful than any other fish, and trout-fishing is within the reach of all. The difficulty is not to

name a river where good sport may be had, but to
name a river where good sport may not be had,
if properly gone about. Railway travelling has
afforded the angler great facilities for the pursuit
of his vocation. One, or at most two hours' ride
will convey all lovers of sport in any large town
in Scotland, and in most of those in England, to
streams where there are plenty of trout; and, to
do them justice, they avail themselves of it to the
utmost. On a holiday the banks of any stream in
the neighbourhood are thickly studded with anglers,
a few of whom meet with good sport, but the greater
number, having demolished their sandwiches and
emptied their flasks, return with their baskets, and
occasionally their heads, lighter than when they left
home. Happily, however, and it is certainly a strong
argument in favour of the attractions of angling,
they are not a whit discouraged; but, on the contrary, eager to return first opportunity, and have
always a good excuse for their want of success. We
never yet met a bad angler that had not a good
excuse; sometimes it is clear water, sometimes a
bright day, sometimes thunder in the air, very often
too many white clouds; and failing all these, there
still remains the great excuse, which is equally applicable to all states of weather and water—that some-
how or other the trout would not take, all of which
we dismiss upon the ground that they should take
the trout. Anglers have also an extraordinary knack
of raising, hooking, and playing, but losing large

trout. The trout once escaped, there is ample scope for the imagination to conjecture its probable size. We have never heard of any phrenologist having made the discovery that persons addicted to angling lack or lose the faculty of correctly distinguishing the essential properties of all matter, number, size, and ponderosity. It is certain, however, that in relation to fish they frequently show a lamentable deficiency in this power. Or, to take the harsher view that we fear finds too much favour with a censorious world, they are in too many cases guilty of habitual and most intolerable exaggerations, not to use a stronger word. We think it a duty on the part of all sober-minded and truthful anglers, to set their faces against this vice, and to expose its "hideous mien" on all occasions. It has brought a stigma on our fraternity ; it has been the cause of many a day's disappointment to believing listeners ; and it has a tendency to propagate itself, for an honestly-disposed angler is often through it himself driven to desert the ways of truth, in order that his "take" may not sink into utter insignificance beside that of a more boastful but less veracious companion. Returning recently from a day's fishing, which had been cut short by a violent thunderstorm, we encountered at the railway station a well-known angler, and waited till the appointed time, well pleased to listen to his pleasant stories about angling, holding a foremost place amongst which were tales of his having detected the frauds and impostures of bragging·brethren. Of his own spoiled sport that day he remarked that he had only caught four trouts, but that they weighed half-a-pound each. The statement naturally excited surprise and suspicion. Such an "average" in that particular stream was unusual on any day ; and on this occasion, as no trout of that size had come our way, or that of the friends who were with us, we had arrived at the conclusion that the "good ones" were sulking, as they will sometimes do. In the railway carriage the man of half-pounders stuck to his statement, but refused to lead evidence by showing his fish. Aided by our friends, however, we succeeded in temporarily poinding his pannier, and dived into its depths. There, amidst boots, stockings, empty flasks, and sandwich papers, we discovered the concealed trouts. Troutkins, rather—not trouts ! Half-pounders !— the whole four together would scarcely have weighed half-a-pound. Whether it was a too lively imagination that had caused the discrepancy between the ideal trouts of the platform and the real trouts of the basket, we care not to inquire ; but we wonder if the same angler will ever again multiply the weight of his take by four, or by any other figure, or whether, made wise by experience, and by this crushing exposure, he will carefully take note of the size of his fish before consigning them to his basket, and not trust to a hasty glance to impress a memory which, let us charitably suppose, may be defective. At all events, people who do not put a padlock on their baskets ought to put one on their mouths.

Some anglers have also a habit of characterising large takes as butchery ; the point where sport stops and butchery commences lying about the individual's greatest take. We cannot see the justice of an opinion that considers the capture of a certain number of trout sport, and of twice that number—taken by the same means—butchery. 'If the sport of angling lies in the capture of fish, it seems evident that the more fish the better sport ; and it is our intention to treat of the different branches of angling solely with the view of showing how the greatest weight of trout can be captured in a given time. There are not many days from May till October, in which an angler, thoroughly versed in all the mysteries of the craft, should not kill at least twelve pounds weight of trout in any county in the south of Scotland, not excepting Edinburghshire itself ; and to describe the way in which this may be done is our object in this small volume.

CHAPTER II.

HE *Salmo fario*, or common trout, is in-
digenous to almost every river, burn, and
loch in Scotland. When in good condition
no tenant of the stream surpasses it in
beauty of appearance. The head is small
and well-shaped, the back finely curved,
and the sides are thickly studded with star-
like spots of a variety of colours, from bright,
red to dark brown. It is singular that it is a
most unusual occurrence to find two trouts spotted
exactly alike, there being generally some difference,
however slight. Why it is so is beyond elucidation,
probably for the same reason that no two human
beings are the same in form and face.

The trout of one stream can sometimes be distinguished from those of another; but this is more
by the complexion and shape, than by any arrangement of the spots; and these are well known to be
entirely the result of feeding, and of the distinctive
characteristics of each stream. Trout taken from a
dark mossy water are dark and ill-coloured, while
those taken from a clear stream are of a correspond-

ing colour. Trout caught under a bank, in the shade of a bush, or in a part of the river where the bottom is dark, are of a darker colour than those caught in the lighter and more open parts; their complexion thus changing according to the colour of the water they inhabit, the colour of the ground over which they move, and the degree of light.

It is not our province to enter into the natural history of the trout, as what anglers wish to know is how to capture them, and we shall therefore consider trout in a purely angling point of view.

With regard to the much-vexed question of whether trout hear or not, naturalists say that they have ears, but we think that these organs are rather intended by nature to convey any agitation in the water, to which they are keenly alive, than external noise. This much seems evident, that no noise out of the water can be heard by a trout in it. Guns have been fired not many yards from trout, but they exhibited no symptoms of alarm, which they would certainly have done had they heard; and, though some English works upon angling caution the angler against speaking aloud at the water-side for fear of alarming the fish, this much is certain, that neither by speaking, nor any other noise the angler can make, is there the least danger of alarming them. They have frequently been caught below a railway bridge at the very time a train was passing overhead.

Those who object to fishing on the ground of

its cruelty have got into nice disquisitions upon the subject of trouts' feelings. Having already referred our readers to Isaac Walton and a learned Doctor of Divinity for the solution of this difficulty, we need not do more than remark that their feelings do not seem to be by any means acute. They have frequently been caught with flies in their mouths which had been left there by some angler a few hours previous. The trout, as Professor Wilson observed, having gone off " with the fly in one cheek and his tongue in the other." A friend of ours met with a remarkable instance of this want of feeling when angling in the Whitadder with worm. He had just made his first cast when a trout went off with the whole apparatus of hook and casting-line. Without moving from where he stood, in the middle of the water, he put on another, and first cast with it caught the trout with the previous casting-line hanging from its mouth, and the hook firmly fixed in it. The vagaries which they exhibit when hooked are usually attributed to pain, but more probably arise from a mixed feeling of surprise and just indignation at having their powers of loco-motion suddenly curtailed.

Of all the senses trout possess, that of sight is the most perfect, and is the one which most affects the angler in pursuit of his vocation. Naturalists say that the appearance and structure of the eye do not lead to the conclusion that their sight is very acute ; but the angler has every reason to believe otherwise. They can detect the smallest fly even in running water; and at night, when it is so dark that the angler cannot see his flies, or even his rod, trout will see and seize a midge-fly, which certainly argues the possession of extraordinary powers of vision. Their eyes are situated in the front of their head, and looking sideways, so that they not only see in front, but also on both sides of them, and even a little behind.

The growth, size, and edible qualities of trout, entirely depend upon the quality and quantity of their food, and these, of course, depend upon the nature of the water they inhabit. The largest and finest trout are usually found in lochs; these yielding more and better food than rivers. The redness in the flesh, which some trout have, is entirely the result of feeding, and is a very good index to their edible qualities. It is quite a common occurrence to capture red and white fleshed trout in the same loch or river; the red fleshed ones being merely better fed specimens of the same kind.

Of rivers, those which flow slowly, and are more like canals than rivers, always produce the best trout. Of this description are most of the English streams; and though trout in some of them are now very scarce, they are occasionally caught of large size; indeed, in point of size, shape, and edible qualities, they bear away the palm from any that can be found in our Scottish streams. Among our own streams of this kind are the Eden and the

Leven in Fifeshire, the Blackadder and the Leet in Berwickshire, the lower parts of the Clyde in Lanarkshire, and Biggar Water in Peeblesshire. All these streams run very slowly; in some of them there are miles where it is difficult to tell at first sight which way the water is flowing. They all contain large, well-shaped, and in general red-fleshed trout, owing to the superior feeding which such streams, running over a bottom of mud or marl, possess, and also to the circumstance that they are generally not numerous. This last fact is due to a number of causes. Deep, slow-running streams are not favourable for spawning, trout requiring shallow water for that purpose. They are also ill-provided with stones and gravel, where the young fry may shelter themselves from their rapacious relatives, and from pike, which generally abound in such places, and commit sad havoc. It is observed that wherever these fresh-water tyrants are found, the trout attain large size, those that escape getting double the quantity of food they would under ordinary circumstances. It seems as if the feeding of a river could only support a certain weight of trout, so that where they are very numerous they are not large, and *vice versa*. Hence proprietors of ponds sometimes drag them with a net, and take out the small fish to improve the size of the remainder.

Of the opposite class from those just mentioned are very rapid streams. Of this kind are most

Highland streams, a few in the hilly parts of the Lowlands, and numerous hill-burns. The rapidity with which their waters run prevents any accumulations taking place which could yield sustenance to the trout, which, in the very height of the season, are poor and soft, and weigh miserably in proportion to their length.

Between the slow-running streams on the one hand, and the very rapid on the other, there is a wide range, comprising all degrees of swiftness; and every angler may get a river in which the variation of stream and pool will be exactly suited to his taste. Like the streams, the trout are of a medium quality, sometimes red in the flesh and sometimes white—depending on the quality and quantity of food they obtain. Of this description are Tweed and its tributaries with few exceptions, most of the streams in the south of Scotland, and a few in the Highlands. In Tweed, trout are occasionally caught six and seven pounds in weight; and we have heard of one being taken from this river of the great weight of twelve pounds, which is the largest river trout we have heard of being caught in Scotland; but they are not of such fine quality as those taken from our smaller streams.

We have mentioned the size of trout as almost entirely depending upon the quantity of their food, without reference to age; indeed this has but little to do with the question, and there being no mark by which their age may be known, any opinion upon this point must be in a great measure conjectured, and cannot well be tested by experiment, as trout will hardly increase in size at all unless free to seek their food and·range the water as they please. We believe that a ten-year old trout may not weigh half-a-pound, or may weigh six pounds, according to the quality and quantity of its food.

The number of trout a river produces depends upon a variety of natural causes, the principal of which is the spawning accommodation. Rivers in which there are plenty of smooth gravelly stretches, and which receive numerous small tributaries, generally produce numbers of trout—shallow water and a gravelly bottom being necessary for the deposit of the spawn. If a river is scantily furnished with spawning accommodation and also with food, the trout will neither be numerous nor large;—the Spey, the Dee, the Esk (Dumfriesshire), and most Highland streams, are examples of this. If the spawning accommodation is deficient and the feeding good, the trout are large, as in most slow running streams. If the spawning accommodation is good and the supply of food limited, the trout are generally numerous but small;—Manor and Quair in Peeblesshire, and some of the tributaries of the Whitadder in Berwickshire, are examples of this, in any of which the angler may easily capture from ten to fifteen dozen of trout any day in summer.

Small rivers produce more trout in proportion to their size than large ones, as a large river has not so much bed in proportion to its volume of water ; and it is principally the bed of a river which yields the insects and other food upon which trout live. Rivers where the salmon-fry, or par, as they are usually called, are very numerous, are rarely such good trouting-streams as those where there are none, these small fish consuming a large proportion of the food of the river. Placing some obstruction at the mouth of a stream, in order to prevent the migratory species from ascending it, would improve materially the size of the common trout it contains. Gala and Leader Waters are examples of this. At the mouths of these streams there are mill-caulds which salmon cannot get over; consequently there are no par, and the trout are much larger than in any similar tributaries of the Tweed where par are to be found. A proprietor on the Leader has been making a well-meant but injudicious attempt to let salmon up, with what success remains to be seen, but in proportion as the salmon get up the trout will diminish in size ; and we think it is not worth while spoiling the trouting qualifications of such a stream as the Leader in order to secure a few ill-conditioned salmon in the end of the season. Clean fish will never ascend so small a stream, and it will afford encouragement to some idle vagabonds to poach in winter.

The trout is unquestionably a voracious feeder, and when hungry is not at all particular as to what it satisfies its appetite upon. Flies and aquatic

insects of all descriptions, minnows and other small
fish, worms, beetles, snails, and frogs, are equally vic-
tims to its rapacity; nor does it feel any compunc-
tions in devouring the smaller members of its own
species. We once, when angling with the minnow
in Leader Water, caught a trout of five or six ounces
in weight with the tail of a fish protruding about
in inch from its mouth, on pulling out which we
found it to be a trout in a partially digested state,
which, when its neighbour swallowed it, must have
weighed at least two ounces. This did not prevent
it from rising at the minnow, but its mouth being
so full it could not get hold of it, and it was only
after repeated rises that it was caught by the outside
of the mouth.

All this might lead to the supposition that trout
would be easily captured; but this is a great error.
Whether it arises from any superior natural endow-
ments, or is merely the result of education, as they
are more fished for than any other fish, and may
from that cause be more wide-awake; this much is
certain that they are the most wary and difficult to
capture of all the inhabitants of the waters, display-
ing a caution and sagacity in taking their food truly
astonishing. They are also the most capricious of
all fish, taking greedily one day what they will
hardly look at the next. The wariness which trout
display varies greatly according to circumstances.
A well-fed trout is at all times more wary than a
half-starved one, as it can afford to allow a suspicious-

looking fly or bait to pass, whereas the other cannot. In rivers much fished, trout, although sometimes numerous, become very shy; seeing artificial flies so often, and being deceived by them, they detect their nature, thus showing that they are, to some extent, possessed of memory.

The only point relating to trout in an angling point of view which remains to be considered, is the season when they are in condition. Generally speaking, they are in condition from the middle or April to the middle of September, but this entirely depends upon the nature of the river and season. They are never in condition till they get abundance of insect food. The supply of this keeps pace with the vegetation on the river's banks, and if the season is advanced, trout, in streams which flow through an early district of country, are quite fit for the table by the beginning of April; if the season is backward, they may be fully a month later of coming into condition. In all streams trout are in their best condition when the May-flies are just done, which is generally about the end of June. They continue in condition all July, but subsequently begin to fall. off—those that are red-fleshed losing their colour, and all kinds becoming pale and soft; and by the end of September or beginning of October are quite full of spawn and hardly worth capturing. It requires very little experience to tell whether or not a trout is in condition; the small head in proportion to the body, and the breadth and thickness of the body itself, at once indicate the well-conditioned fish. All anglers should confine their operations to that period of the year when trout are fit for the table, as it is unsportsman-like in the highest degree to kill fish that are of no use. Such being our opinion, we shall limit the consideration of angling to the months in which trout are in condition.

During the last twenty years a great decrease has taken place in the quantity of trout in our southern streams, and any angler who has been in the habit of frequenting regularly a particular stream during that time must have noticed an almost annual diminution in the number, and still more in the size, of its finny inhabitants. This is an alarming fact, and well worthy of the attention of the angling community, as some of the most fruitful causes of this disastrous result might be stopped. Some of them, however, there is no help for, and the most prejudicial of these is the drainage of the land, more particularly of the hill-pastures for sheep. So long as drainage was confined to the rivers' banks, its effects were not so observable ; but now that it has extended to the recesses of the mountains, whence most of our rivers receive nine-tenths of their water, and every hill, glen, and moor, is drained, it tells severely upon the streams and their inhabitants. The water, which used to find its way to the rivers gradually, keeping them large and full for a considerable time, is now conducted to them very soon after the rain falls, and runs off in a day or two, leaving them clear and dwindled till the next flood.

Several old residents on Tweedside have assured us, that fifty years ago, when there was a flood, Tweed continued the dark porter colour, so highly prized by anglers, for a week or more, and then ran clear but pretty full. Now, the flood is very heavy for the first day or two, and then falls rapidly, in three or four days becoming quite clear, and for weeks scarcely half the size of what it used to be when at its smallest.

It is supposed that the heavy floods we now have shift the gravel, and carry off a large quantity of the spawn of the trout, and also of the eggs of aquatic insects. Then, again, when the waters are very small, the eggs of aquatic insects are left dry, and their vitality destroyed, so that the number of insects upon which trout feed is materially lessened, and at the same time the number and size of trout, which, as has just been stated, depends in a great measure upon the quantity of food. If drainage, for which there is no remedy, has such an injurious effect, there is the more necessity for looking after the causes which might be stopped; and the worst of these are the manufactories, bleachfields, etc., which are so thickly studded along the banks of our southern streams, and which send their dyes and other deleterious refuse straight into the streams, causing sad havoc. When we mentioned this in our first edition, the *Border Advertiser* came down upon us as having fallen into " the vulgar or rather urbane error, that manufactories injured the fishing." It would be worse than useless to argue the point with a man living upon the banks of Gala Water. If Gala Water from Galashiels to Tweed, which, to use the words of - Mr. Stoddart, " is an unseemly ditch, full of the blackest and most noxious dyes," and which the *Border Advertiser* must see and smell daily, will not convince him, no argument will. Why, the " Man of Ross," who has propounded the rather startling theory that grilse are not young salmon, and whose theory *Blackwood's Magazine* has settled for ever, labours under no such hallucination as our friend the *Advertiser*. That manufactories, however, do injure the fishing, all England proves ; there, the refuse from them and the drainage of towns are conveyed into the streams, and the result is that salmon are not, and trout are fast going. Even in Scotland several streams have suffered severely from these causes, and they are daily increasing. The following graphic, and we fear prophetic, foreshadowing of the fate of Tweed, is taken from the *Quarterly Review* for January 1857, and is written by an angler no less celebrated for wielding the rod than the pen :—

" Look at what the Tweed is now in contrast with what will be its look and smell at that not distant *then*. See her and hers rolling along, beautiful and beautifying, through regions where every ruin is history, and every glen is song, gathering her

tributes from a thousand hills—from where sweet
Teviot sings, unceasingly, its ' farewell to Cheviot's
mountains blue ;' where pensive Yarrow winds like
a silver chain, amid ' the dowie dens,' where, in the
sad and silent ' Forest '

> ' The wildered Ettrick wanders by,
> Loud murmuring to the careless morn,'

till, grown stately, massive, and brimming, ' Tweed's
fair river, broad and deep,' wheeling beneath the
donjon keep of Norham and the battlements of
Berwick, sinks into the ocean as glittering pure as
when she broke away from her native hills. Is all
this to vanish, and in its place a pestilential sewer ?
Is that which spreads health and beauty around to
become an eyesore, extending over half the breadth
of Scotland ? Shall the turrets of Abbotsford be
reflected from a monster gutter, all stains and stench?
Shall fair Melrose, instead of being ' viewed aright
by the pale moonlight,' be nosed in the dark ?
Forbid it, all the powers of Parliament ! If, indeed, that prohibition could not be uttered without
destroying or impeding the brisk and cheerful in-
dustry which has sprung up among these sweet
hills, there might be nothing for it but to sigh and
submit. But it would be almost profane to doubt
that from so great an evil there must be means of
escape—that Hawick may prosper, and yet Tweed
be preserved."

If trout alone were concerned, there is little
doubt that they would be left to their fate, and

come to an ignominious, unhonoured, but not un-mourned-for end ; but now that valuable property in the salmon-fishings is imperilled, there seems some prospect that the powers of Parliament, which have been so pathetically appealed to, may interfere.

Another of the most fruitful causes of the depopulation of our streams is netting, and it has greatly increased of late years. The rivers are now so exceedingly small during summer, that they afford every facility for the successful practice of this illegal method of catching trout. The net used for this purpose is what is usually called " the harry-water net." Nets of this kind are made so light that they can be carried in the pocket, and so com-plete in structure, that a whole pool may be almost cleaned of its finny inhabitants at a single haul. Tweed and its tributaries suffer more from netting than any other streams in Scotland, and it is most usually carried on in the neighbourhood of towns or villages, where the poachers can find a ready sale for their trout.

There are three remedies which might be adopted to prevent netting. The first, and undoubtedly the most efficacious of these, is to have the rivers watched ; but this is so expensive as to render it quite impracticable. Another way is to drive stakes into the principal pools and streams, which would prevent nets being drawn through. During the last few years this has been tried, and we understand with great success, in some streams in the neighbourhood of Hawick. Gala Water was also staked last summer, and an association formed for the protection of the river, called the Gala Angling Association, which every angler who visits that stream should join. It is, however, too soon yet to speak of the effects of this upon Gala, but we have no doubt it will prove highly beneficial. Stakes, however, are liable to this objection, that they interfere with the angler while landing a fish, or when using the worm. The last and most feasible plan is to put large stones in the water, which would have the same effect as the stakes, and would not, like them, interfere with the angler, and would also afford shelter to the fish. The last reason we shall assign for the decrease of trout is the enormous increase of anglers of late years ; there are twenty anglers now for one there was fifty years ago. A gentleman who resided on Tweedside about the beginning of the present century, says that he and one or two others were the only anglers in a district comprising many miles of water. Then, when a flood came, Tweed remained large for ten days, and was swarming with trout so unwary that they could be caught with tackle and flies which a modern angler would reject as totally useless. Look at the state of the case now. How widely different ! Every villager has a rod, and uses it, with more effect too than most amateur anglers ; and it is not at all uncommon to be unable of an evening to get a single pool or stream to yourself ; and on a favourable day in the month of May, "Tweed's fair river, broad and deep," will be fished by many hundred followers of the gentle craft. Now, as almost all these catch a few trout, and some of them catch large basketsful, it is obvious that this must diminish the number of trout. The present scarcity of trout is forcing itself upon the attention of anglers, and it is sometimes suggested that trout should get a jubilee ; but apart frem the impossibility of ever carrying such a design into execution, this is un-necessary ; if net-fishing was entirely stopped, the streams would quickly regain a portion at least of their old fame. The trout taken by the rod in some districts are often few compared with those taken by the net. It is not by the dozen, nor yet by the basketful, that net-fishers count their spoils, but by the hundredweight, and this, of course, must speedily thin the trout in any stream, however prolific it may be.

Fair rod-fishing will never seriously injure a stream. Of this Gala Water affords an excellent illustration. The favourite resort of anglers from Edinburgh, it is fished during the angling season by about thirty anglers daily, and supposing they only average two pounds each, it implies the capture of an immense quantity of trout. It also suffers as much from nets as any tributary of the Tweed, and yet in those parts where nets cannot be successfully wrought trout are still numerous. Nor are they by any means contemptible in size ; in this respect they will bear comparison with any of the other tributaries of Tweed open to the public. We once took with the minnow, between Bowland and Stow, twenty trout, the whole we got that day, which weighed fifteen pounds, and we never got such a large average size of trout in any of the other tributaries of the Tweed, or even in Tweed itself.

There are not by any means too many anglers; on the contrary, our Scottish waters would accommodate, if properly distributed, twenty times as many as there now are. Tweed and its tributaries alone would, giving each plenty of water to himself, accommodate several thousands every day during the season.

Much fishing, besides to a certain extent thinning the trout, operates against the angler's killing large takes by making the remaining trout more wary; and it is more from this cause than from the scarcity of trout, that so many anglers return unsuccessful from much-fished streams. The waters also now remain brown-coloured for such a short time that the modern angler is deprived, unless on rare occasions, of even this aid to his art of deception; and the clearness of the water and the increased wariness of the trout are the main causes why the tackle of fifty years ago would be found so faulty now. Fifty years ago it was an easy thing to fill a basket with trout, not so now; then there were ten trout for one there is now —the colour of the water favoured the angler, and the trout were comparatively unsophisticated; now filling a basket with trout, at least in some of our southern streams open to the public, when they are low and clear, is a feat of which any angler may be proud. To do so he must oppose craft to craft, and cunning to cunning, and must study very closely the habits and instincts of the trout. Angling is in fact every day becoming more difficult, and consequently better worthy of being followed as a scientific amusement. So far from looking upon the increase of anglers with alarm, it ought to be regarded with satisfaction : the more trout are fished for, the more wary they become ; the more wary they are, the more skill is required on the angler's part ; and as the skill an amusement requires constitutes one of its chief attractions, angling is much better sport now than it was fifty years ago.

CHAPTER III.

RESS.—The only advice it is necessary to give the angler on this head is, not to select any very gaudy colours, and to avoid any approach to foppery, as trout have the most thorough contempt for a fop, and will not on any account allow themselves to be handled with kid gloves. Nothing is so completely out of place at the water-side as an individual got up with all the elaboration of one of *Punch's* swells. We often wonder what has tempted such an one to leave off sunning himself in Princes Street to astonish the inhabitants of some distant stream. Seriously speaking, however, gaudy colours are apt to attract the notice of the trout, and are perceived by them at a greater distance. Some anglers may think this is being unnecessarily particular; but on a sunny day, when to escape observation the angler will require to crawl up the river's bank, dress becomes a subject of some importance. Every angler ought to furnish himself with a waterproof coat; they are now made so light that they can be put in the pocket or strapped to the basket, without the least inconvenience. Some anglers, who, we suppose, must belong to the new school of muscular Christians, allege they never feel comfortable till they get wet ; but if, as we suppose, the greater number never feel comfortable when they do, a' waterproof coat, a wide-awake hat, and wading-boots, will render them quite independent of the weather.

Wading Boots and Stockings.—Anglers who can stand knee-deep in water for a whole day during any part of the angling season without any danger of suffering from it, require nothing to wade with but a pair of good stout shoes or boots. If the water is very cold, wearing two pairs of stockings instead of one will add to the angler's comfort. Many anglers, however, particularly those whose mode of life is sedentary, cannot expose themselves to wet with any degree of impunity, so that they must either refrain from wading or wear waterproofs of some description. The ordinary leather boots, such as are generally worn by fishermen, are undoubtedly the most substantial article of the kind to be had. The only objection to them, and it is certainly a serious one, is their great weight ; the lightest of them when properly ironed weighing four or five pounds each. To leather wading-boots we prefer waterproof stockings, which are now made light as well as substantial, and may be procured at a very moderate price. These waterproof stockings are intended to be worn over the ordinary worsted ones; some even wear two pairs of stockings below them to keep their feet warm in cold weather. Between the waterproof stockings and the boots, to prevent the latter from cutting the former, another pair of worsted stockings must be put.

Waterproof stockings will last a long time, if, after having been used, they are turned inside out to allow the perspiration which accumulates in the inside to dry off, otherwise it will cause the material to rot. Over them the angler should have a pair of good stout shoes or boots well ironed. In all boots or shoes meant for wading this should be attended to, or the angler may slip among the stones, and get an unexpected bath some morning. It will also be found an improvement to bore holes in the soles of them to permit the water to escape, as much water about the feet is disagreeable as well as weighty; and wading gear of any description is quite heavy enough in itself. To keep wading boots and shoes soft, and prevent the leather from cracking, it is necessary that when drying they should be well greased. For this purpose we know nothing better than the grease which curriers use for their leather, and which may be had at any currier's.

Rods.—There is no article of an angler's equipment that affords more room for the exercise of taste in its selection than the rod. Rods may be bought at such a moderate price, and withal so much better than any angler can make them for himself,

that it is unnecessary to give any instructions for
the mechanical part of rod-making, and we shall
merely mention what a good rod should be made of,
and the qualities it should possess. The two great
requisites in a rod we consider to be stiffness and
lightness, two qualities exceedingly difficult to com-
bine. The amount of stiffness should be such that,
when casting, the forward motion of the rod may be
stopped pretty quickly without any recoil of the
point taking place. Most of the rods that are to be
had ready made in Edinburgh are useless from their
excessive pliability, and from what we have seen of
English and Irish rods they are still worse. This is
not the fault of the rod-makers who require to suit
the public taste, but the fault of anglers who will
have their rods made in that manner. We know of
no place where a better rod can be made than in
Edinburgh, if the angler only says that he wishes it
stiff. In casting with a supple rod, after propelling
the line forward, and stopping the forward motion
of the hand, a recoil of the point takes place, which,
to a considerable extent, interferes with the forward
motion of the line.

The advantages of a stiff rod are its great superiority in casting; it will throw a longer and a
lighter line, and with greater certainty, to any spot
the angler wishes. Its advantages, in these respects,
are particularly apparent in a windy day, when it is
necessary to cast against the wind, or even sideways
to it. With a supple rod, in such circumstances,

it is almost impossible to get the line out at all. Another great advantage of a stiff rod is its superiority in striking. In striking, by a quick motion of the wrist, the angler moves the rod; if this is done with a supple rod, the part of it in the hand is moved immediately, but not so the point; the rod yields throughout; and the point, by means of which the line is pulled, may almost be said to remain stationary for a moment after striking, and then moves in a slow, uncertain manner; very different from the instantaneous sharp strike of a good stiff rod.

Lightness we consider an essential qualification in a rod; the lighter it is, the angler can cast it the oftener, and use it the longer at a time. This, however, is a matter which the angler should regulate for himself, as a rod that will be too heavy for one will be a mere whip in the hands of another.

The butts of rods are frequently made hollow to contain one or more spare points; and to such as have their points made very thin, this is almost indispensable, as it is by no means uncommon for some anglers to demolish one or two of these flimsy articles in a day. If the butt-piece is to be made hollow, it should be made of ash; the boring of it is a very difficult process, and can only be done by a machine. Saplings are also sometimes used for this purpose, in the centre of which there is generally a considerable quantity of pith, which can easily be scooped out, and the hollow space enlarged. We are by no means partial to hollow butts; they require to be made so thick that they destroy the symmetry of the rod, and they never bend from the hand as a well-made rod should. It is only in Scotland that hollow butts are much used. English anglers object to them as destroying the bend of a rod, and carry a spare point in the handle of their landing-net, which is made hollow for that purpose ; in our opinion, a great improvement upon the hollow butts. The necessity for spare points would be avoided, if anglers would get their rods made stronger. A moderately stout rod made of good material, with plenty of rings, will stand much more than could be supposed from its appearance, and even if it should break, it can be temporarily repaired in a very short time. If the butt is not made hollow, fir may be substituted for ash with advantage, as it is much lighter, and quite strong enough.

For the middle pieces of a rod, there is nothing like hickory ; it possesses elasticity and strength in a great degree, and, if properly taken care of, will stand long and frequent use. Good hickory is the most valuable of all woods to the rod-maker.

The tops of rods are made of a great many different kinds of wood — hickory, bamboo, lance, log-wood, greenheart, and numerous others. The two last mentioned are too brittle and too heavy, pressing severely upon the middle pieces, and causing that excessive pliancy which spoils a rod for all useful purposes. Lance, though not so brittle, is open to the latter objection, and if used at all, should be used very sparingly. Hickory and bamboo, particularly the latter, are best suited for tops, and we think the greater part, if not the whole, should be made of bamboo. The strength of bamboo lies in the skin, and in order to turn this to the best account, rod-makers lay two or three slits together, so as to form a complete skin all round. This is much more troublesome than making it of one piece, but is more durable, and with good usage will never break. Rods are sometimes made entirely of bamboo, but they possess no advantage over those in common use, to compensate for the additional expense—a twelve-foot rod of this material costing £3 or £4. For our own use we are exceedingly partial to rods made entirely of cane, with the exception of the top, which is bamboo. They are stiff, strong, and very light ; the only objection to them is, that they are liable to take a bend, unless the angler takes care to straighten the pieces before putting them past.

Great diversity of opinion exists as to how the different pieces of a rod should be put together when intended to be used. Some anglers, ourselves included, prefer the tie system, for the following reasons :—A tied rod is not nearly so liable to break as one with brass joints ; the wood of a rod requires to be thinned in order to put the brass on, rendering them liable to give way at the joints—a fact which the experience of all anglers will confirm. A tied

rod also bends most equally throughout ; and no
angler will deny that it is the most agreeable to use.
The great objection, however, to brass joints is, that,
in order to bear their weight, the rod requires to be
made so much thicker throughout.   A rod of twelve
feet, without brass joints, should weigh about fourteen ounces ; with brass joints, it will weigh about
a pound and a half, nearly double the weight, which
tells fearfully upon the angler's arm in fly-fishing.
When the tie system is adopted, the splices should
be well waxed, as also the thread with which they
are tied, otherwise they will be constantly slipping.
This mode of joining is objected to by some on the
ground that there is a good deal of time spent in
putting the rod up ; but we think much more time
will be lost by using a rod with the additional weight
necessary to stand brass joints.

If the angler cannot be troubled to tie the pieces
of his rod together, joints of some kind are indispensable.   The old mode of joining was by screw joints ;
but they do not last, and the plain slip joint has
entirely superseded them, and is undoubtedly the
most convenient and lasting method of putting a rod
together.   The pieces are the better of being tied
together, as, if they are not, they may slip.   For
this purpose, small wire catches should be put at
the bottom and top of each piece.

A well-made rod, when put up, should yield
slightly from a little above the hand to the top, and
if intended to be used with one hand should balance

about a foot above the hand ; if intended to be used with both hands, about a foot further up. The facility of casting with a well-balanced rod is very great, as the part of the rod below the hand acts as a lever.

The reel is usually attached to the rod by rings, which is undoubtedly the most convenient plan, as it can be taken off at pleasure. In a one-handed rod, the reel should be as close to the butt end as possible, as its leverage will be greater there ; in a double-handed rod, sufficient room must be left below the reel for the hand. When the weight of the butt end and reel together are not in themselves sufficient to balance a rod, lead should be added till it balance at the proper place.

Rings are indispensable to a rod in order to convey the line from the reel to the point. A difference of opinion exists as to whether they should be fixed or moveable. For our part, if they could be fixed so as not to move, we would prefer them that way, as they let off the line much more easily ; but they generally have just sufficient stiffness to be troublesome. When they come into contact with anything, they are knocked over and remain so; and unless the angler notice it, the first fish will break his line.

When treating of the different branches of angling, we will mention the size and description of rod most suitable for each ; but the size of rod we have advocated for fly-fishing is so much shorter than

usual, that it may with great propriety be objected
to, as being unsuitable for any other kind of fishing,
To obviate this as much as possible, we have a joint
made in our fly-rod about a foot from the butt-end,
and carry with us a spare butt of about four feet in
length. This can be attached to the basket without
the angler suffering the least inconvenience, or may
be made with joints, which will render it more por-
table. When wishing to change from fly to bait, we
take off the short butt and put on the long one, and
have then a rod suitable for any purpose.

To keep a rod in good order, and render it im-
pervious to wet, it should be varnished occasionally.
If any part of it is made of bamboo, this should be
done every three or four times it is used, as the
varnish will not adhere to the skin of the cane, but
cracks off in casting. For this purpose spirit varnish
is generally used, which may be had of any fishing-
tackle maker or druggist, and should be applied with
a brush.

Reels.—The best reels are those made of brass,
and with a plain wheel. Some anglers prefer the
multiplier, because it rolls up the line more quickly,
and others the rack, because it presents a greater
resistance to the running off of the line; but these
advantages are counterbalanced by their liability to
go wrong, particularly the multiplier; and we have
known anglers who have lost a salmon by the rack
catching at a critical moment. A plain wheel will
sometimes allow the line to run off too freely, but this

is the angler's fault, who, in playing a trout, should regulate the amount of stress to be laid on it by the hand entirely. Reels have been greatly improved in shape of late years; they are now made much deeper, and not so broad, thus allowing the line to be run off more easily, and be wound up more quickly. The size of the reel should always bear some proportion to the size of the rod. A large reel seems quite out of place on a small rod, and *vice versa.*

Lines are now usually made by a machine, and if care be taken in their construction, they can be made much better in this manner than by the hand. They can be bought at such a moderate price, that it is not worth any angler's trouble making them for himself. They are made of horse-hair, or a mixture of hair and silk; those made of hair entirely are more durable than any other kind, as they are not so liable to rot as all lines are of which silk forms a component part. The latter, however, are stronger for their bulk, and are much more easily thrown— two considerable advantages. Lines made entirely of silk, prepared in some patent manner, are now in very common use, and seem likely to supersede every other kind. They are very strong, and are more easily thrown than any kind of line, but like all lines made of silk, they will rot unless dried after being wet. As to the length of line, the angler should be guided entirely by the size of the river he intends fishing in. For small streams, twenty yards will be quite sufficient, but in first-class rivers and lochs three times that quantity will be necessary. .

After the ordinary winch-line, it is usual to have a casting-line of horse-hair loosely twisted, or triple gut. Some anglers prefer the hair because they think it lighter, which, however, is a mistake, as gut is stronger for its weight than any material the angler can use, and is also heavier for its bulk, which is a great assistance to casting.

Gut.—This article is made from the entrails of the silk worm before it casts its silk, and is principally manufactured in Spain, Portugal, Italy, and Sicily. Of all the materials used by the angler, it is the one which it is most difficult to procure good, and which it is most necessary should be so. For angling in clear water, inhabited by cunning cautious trout, *fine thin gut is absolutely necessary for success*, and we think that anglers in Scotland are in general not sufficiently aware of the importance of fine gut. An immense quantity is imported annually, put up in hanks of about a hundred threads each. So far as we can judge, a good deal appears to be spoilt in the manufacture. As it is made at present, nine hanks out of ten are totally unfit for fine trouting purposes, and even the very finest hanks seldom contain more than twenty threads fit for dressing flies or bait-hooks upon. The first angler who travels in Spain should try to prevail upon the Spaniards to pay a little more attention to the manufacture of this article ; it would amply repay them for their trouble, as they would get three times the price for it. Meantime all anglers should use none but the very finest threads, and if they continue doing so, coarse gut will become valueless, and the demand will soon influence the manufacture. We are informed by an importer that gut used to be made much better, but that the price has fallen so low, that it will not remunerate for the trouble required to make it fine ; so that anglers have themselves to blame.

The qualities good gut should possess are roundness, transparency, and thinness. Unless gut is round it glitters in the sun, which renders it useless to the angler ; it must also be perfectly free from that white glossy appearance which round gut frequently has, and which renders it more easily seen than clear gut of twice the thickness. Thinness, however, is the great desideratum, as the thinner it is there is the less chance of the trout detecting it. Some anglers, particularly those in the north, seem to think that gut cannot be had too thick, whereas the reverse is the case—it cannot be had too fine.

Of late years, fishing-tackle manufacturers have been in the habit of reducing the size of gut, which is done by drawing it through a machine, and paring away a considerable portion of the gut. By this means it may be made of any thinness, but it injures the texture of the gut, and destroys its transparency, and it is certainly better if it can be had sufficiently fine without reducing. Gut prepared in this manner is also very expensive ; costing from ten to six-teen shillings a hank.

All gut is more or less of a clear colour, which glitters in the sun, and in order to divest it of this it requires to be stained. The colour of the dye used is of little consequence ; the object being to render it of a dull colour, and this may be best accomplished by dying it of a bluish-green. This dye may be made by boiling a handful of logwood in a pint of water, and adding copperas till it is of the required colour. A piece of copperas about half the size of a pea will be sufficient ; if too much is put in it will make it quite blue. The gut should be put into the liquid when cold, and allowed to remain till it is of the required colour.

Gut plays a very important part in the formation of all trouting tackle : hooks of every description should be dressed upon it ; and all casting-lines, and, indeed, every part of the line that is intended to touch the water, should be made of this material.

After the ordinary winch-line, there should be a casting-line composed of seven or eight lengths of triple gut twisted together. This can only be done properly by a machine for the purpose, which may be had in any fishing-tackle shop. Only the longest threads should be selected for this purpose, and they should be as nearly as possible of one thickness. Before attaching them to the machine, they should be soaked in cold water for half-an-hour, or they will be certain to break. After the lengths are twisted, they may be joined together according to the angler's taste, taking care that they taper from one end to the other. The most secure method of joining them is with the single slip-knot, lapping the ends over with well-waxed silk thread ; a little spirit varnish makes all secure. Another way of joining them is by whipping the ends together with silk ; this is the neater plan of the two, but it is continually giving way, and requires to be done over again ; so that, unless the angler makes up his own tackle, he will find it exceedingly troublesome ; anglers practising this method should always keep the joinings well varnished. After the triple gut-line, there should be four or five lengths of picked gut, tapered in thickness to where the fly or bait tackle is attached ; these should be joined together by a common knot. Instead of fastening the fly or bait cast to this by a loop, as is usually done, it is better to fasten it by a knot, as it is neater, and makes less show in the water.

There is nothing so apt to slip as gut, and therefore the knot by which to tie the threads together is of some importance. The water-knot is made by laying the two ends together, rolling them round the forefinger of the left hand, and passing one thread and the adjoining end through the loop thus formed ; this is called the single water-knot, and is very neat, but apt to slip. The double water-knot is done in the same way; but the ends are passed twice through instead of once, making a very firm knot, but rather

clumsy.   The single slip-knot is made by laying the
ends together, and simply knotting the one round the
other ; in the right direction it will hold together,
but may be separated by pulling the short ends.   The
double slip-knot is so far the same ; but in knotting
the threads round each other, the ends are passed
twice through instead of once: this, if properly done,
makes a neat and firm joining, and is the one we
always use.   Before knotting, gut should be well
soaked in cold water.

Hooks.—The two great points to be attended to
in the selection of hooks are the bend, and the temper and durability of the wire.   Great diversity of
opinion exists as to what sort of bend is best adapted
for hooking, and in order to please every one, a
variety of bends are made ; these are the round,
Limerick, Kirby, and sneck bends.   The two last
may be dismissed at once, as they are not a whit
better adapted for hooking than the ordinary round
bend, and are much more difficult to bait.   The main
point, as we have already stated, being to hook a
fish, the round bend appears to be the best adapted
for that purpose.   It is an error to suppose, that
because the point of the Limerick is more turned
out, it is therefore more likely to take a hold when
the angler strikes ; on the contrary, the more the
point of the hook is turned out, the less is the chance
of hooking ; there is certainly a greater probability
of the point of the hook coming into contact with the
mouth of the fish, but it merely grazes it, and then

starts off. The reason of this is, that when the angler pulls, the pressure upon the point does not pull it straight in, but sideways. The accompanying illustration will assist to explain this.

No. 1.   No. 2.

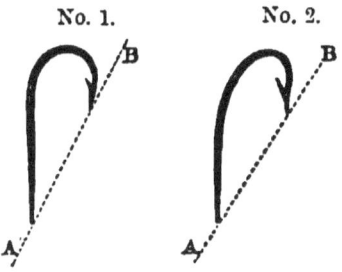

No. 1 is a round bent hook of the shape we use ; and No. 2 is a Limerick of the ordinary bend. When the point of a hook comes in contact with anything, the line being attached to the end of the shank, the pressure takes place in the direction of the straight line B A, so that in No. 1 the pressure will be almost in the same direction as the point ; whereas in No. 2 it will be very nearly at right angles to the point, requiring three times the force to fix it, and rendering it exceedingly liable to start off and merely graze the mouth of the fish. As a proof of this, if the angler is using hooks which are not sufficiently tempered, he will frequently, after having fished for some time, find them bent out in the point, showing that the pull was so much off the straight line, that the force which was sufficient to bend the wire was not enough to fix the hook. Whenever this is observed, the angler should restore the hook to its original shape by biting it between his teeth, as it will never catch a fish in that state. The point of the hook must not lie in exactly the same line as B A, because if it does, when it comes in contact with the mouth of a fish it will hardly take any hold at all; it must be so much off the line B A, that when it comes against anything it will press into it. In order to understand what we mean, the reader should take two dressed hooks of the same shapes as Nos. 1 and 2, and pull them against some soft substance, when he will at once see the force of these remarks.

We believe that with a fly dressed upon a hook of No. 1 bend, we could catch at least three trout for two we could catch with a fly dressed on a hook bent as No. 2, out of an equal number of rises. There are numbers of anglers who are of the same opinion, and would not use a Limerick hook on any account; and we have met with professional anglers, ready enough in general to accept of any kind of tackle, who absolutely refused to take Limerick hooks, as being of no use. Some anglers shorten the shanks of their hooks considerably, but this is highly objectionable, as it has exactly the same effect as having the point turned out, and, if carried to any extent, renders the chances of hooking a trout exceedingly small.

The round bent hooks manufactured by Bartlett and Son, and Addlington and Hutchinson, can generally be depended upon for temper and durability of wire. The hooks of neither of these makers are exactly of the proper shape, being rather too much turned out in the points. Addlington's small sizes are, without exception, the best that are made, as they neither bend nor break, but are somewhat difficult to get, as few fishing-tackle makers keep them. Bartlett's small sizes are liable to bend (a very bad fault), but the same objection does not apply to his large sizes, which we prefer to Addlington's, the latter maker's hooks, from No. 9 upwards, being too thick in the wire. It is a great improvement to get them japanned in the same way as the Limerick hooks, for if left with the blue steel exposed they are exceedingly liable to rust.

Bartlett numbers his hooks from $1\frac{1}{2}$, the largest size, to 17, the smallest. Addlington's numbers are from the largest trouting size to 00, the smallest. Being better acquainted with Bartlett's hooks than any others, when we speak of hooks in the subsequent parts of this volume the reader will understand that it is his sizes to which we allude. The following numbers of Bartlett and Addlington are about the same size :—

Bartlett's Nos. .	1	2	3	4	5	6	7	8	9	10	11	12	13	14
Addlington's Nos.	12	11	10	9	8	7	6	5	4	3	2	1	0	00

Basket - pannier or Creel.—The most elegantly shaped baskets are those made of split willows, usually called " French made." For the size of basket every angler should be guided by the quantity of fish he expects to capture ; nothing looks worse than a few trout half-hidden with grass in the

E

bottom of a large basket. It will be found an improvement to attach a strap to the back of the basket, by which the angler may strap on his waterproof coat; this has the double advantage of being the most convenient mode of carrying it, and of acting as a kind of cushion between the basket and the back.

Landing or Minnow Net.—The meshes of the landing-net should be made sufficiently small to admit of its being employed for capturing minnows. Nets are not much used in Scotland for landing trout, as our rivers in general have plenty of smooth sloping banks, and using a net in such would rather diminish the pleasure of landing a fish. But in lochs a landing-net is indispensable, and even in rivers, if the banks are steep, or the sides weedy, it will be found a very great convenience. Under any circumstances, if the angler has an attendant to carry his basket—which we strongly advise all who angle for pleasure to have—he should have a landing-net with him, as even though he should not require it for trout he may meet with a shoal of minnows, and feel disposed to try minnow-fishing. Nets are now made with jointed hoops, which fold up and can be put in the basket or pocket; the handles also are made with numerous joints, or in telescope fashion—the one slipping into the other—so that they take up very little room.

Fishing Pocket-Book.—In order to afford ample room for the accommodation of every kind of tackle, this article should be large—at least six or seven inches long by five or six wide. It should have numerous pockets, and also divisions of parchment to keep the tackle separate. Keeping flies in a book squeezes and destroys them, and the preferable plan is to keep them in an oblong tin box, which should be from five to six inches long by four or five wide, and which may be made with a division in the middle and to open at both sides ; it should also be furnished with slips of paper to keep the fly-casts separate.

Lastly, in regard to tackle, we advise anglers, before putting past flies or lines, to dry them previously, and to have everything connected with their angling equipment of the very best material ; it will be found a great assistance to successful fishing, and also the most economical plan in the end.

CHAPTER IV.

LY-FISHING has always been, and we believe always will be, the favourite method of angling; and deservedly so. Few who have once owned its sway are capable of resisting its attractions. What golden memories of the past it recals! What bright visions of the future it portrays! And when May comes, that month pre-eminently the fly-fisher's, with its bright sunny mornings and soft southern breezes, once more, unencumbered with anything save a light rod and small box of flies, the angler wends his way to some favourite stream. Once more with elastic tread he climbs the mountain's brow, and having gained the summit, what a' prospect meets his gaze! There, far as the eye can reach, rises into the blue sky summit after summit of the heath-clad hills, while underneath lie the grassy slope and luxuriant meadow, the green corn-field and waving wood, and winding and circling among all like a silver thread lies the far-stretching stream in all its beauty. There is nothing to break the solitude save the plaintive bleating of the sheep or the cry of the moorcock. As the angler descends, the music of the song-bird meets his ear from every bush, and the groves resound with the cooing of the wood-pigeon or the soft notes of the cuckoo. And now he approaches the scene of his anticipated triumph. There are the deep rocky pool and racing shallow, the whirling eddy and rippling stream. Now it pauses as if to enjoy the glory of the prospect, then rushes impetuously forward, as if eager to drink in the grandeur of some new scene. Now it foams over rocks, and then meanders slowly between green banks. Everything seems endowed with life to welcome the return of summer. The very river is alive with leaping trout. Everything tends to cheer the angler's heart and encourage his hopes. No wonder that with Sir Henry Wotton he finds "fly-fishing" a "cheerer of the spirits, a tranquilliser of the mind, a calmer of unquiet thoughts, a diverter of sadness."

And then the art itself is lively and graceful. Look at the angler as he approaches some favourite spot. See him as he observes the monarch of the pool regaling himself on the incautious insect that sports in fancied security upon the surface. Inwardly he vows that it shall be avenged. Cautiously he approaches, concealing himself by kneeling or keeping behind some bush, lest by any chance his expected prey should discover him and so be warned. Gracefully wheeling his long line behind, he lays his flies down softly as a snow-flake just above the desired spot. A moment of expectancy succeeds, the flies approach the very place where the trout was last seen. Look at the angler how with keen eye he watches, to strike with alert hand the moment he either feels or sees the least movement. There is a stoppage of the line and an instantaneous movement of the angler's wrist and the trout is fast. At first he shakes his head as if surprised and be-wildered at the unwonted interference with his liberty, but gradually awakening to a sense of the danger of his position, he collects his scattered energies and makes a gallant fight for liberty; frequently he will leap in the air several times as if to ascertain the character of his opponent, and then make a frantic rush; but the figure on the bank follows him like a shadow, and at last, strength and hope both exhausted, he turns on his side and be-comes an easy prey, leaving the angler to contem-plate the speckled sides of his captive with satisfac-tion, and to congratulate himself on having achieved such a feat with a tiny hook and tackle like a gos-samer.

The victory, however, is not always with the angler—more frequently the other way; often at the last moment, just as he is putting out his hand to secure his prize, the trout makes a bolt and is gone, leaving the disappointed artist the picture of blank dismay, and in a very unenviable frame of mind; indeed, of all the trials of the temper which

occur in the ordinary course of life, there is none to
compare with that of losing a good trout at the last
moment, and anglers have various ways of giving
vent to their pent-up feelings, depending upon their
peculiar idiosyncrasy. But of all the different means
of relief there is perhaps none at once so satisfactory
and so reprehensible as that referred to by a late
great humorist, who, if not an angler, was the friend
and associate of anglers :—

> " The flask frae my pocket
>   I poured into the socket,
> For I was provokit unto the last degree ;
>   And to my way o' thinkin',
>   There's naething for 't but drinkin',
> When a trout he lies winkin' and lauchin' at me."

Everything combines to render fly-fishing the
most attractive of all the branches of the angler's
art. The attempt to capture trout which are seen to
rise at natural flies is in itself an excitement which
no other method possesses. Then the smallness of
the hook and the fineness of the tackle necessary
for success increase the danger of escape, and consequently the excitement and pleasure of the capture ;
and for our own part we would rather hook, play,
and capture a trout of a pound weight with fly than
one of a pound and half with minnow or worm,
where the hooks being larger there is less chance of
their losing their hold, and the gut being stronger
there is less risk of its breaking. Fly-fishing is also
the cleanest and most elegant and gentlemanly of

all the methods of capturing trout. The angler who practises it is saved the trouble of working with worms, of catching, keeping alive, and salting minnows, or searching the river's banks for the natural insect. Armed with a light single-handed rod and a few flies ·he may wander from county to county, and kill trout wherever they are to be found.

One advantage fly-fishing possesses above any other mode is, that it is equally applicable to all waters, be they silent lakes, slow-running rivers, or roaring streams, rendering it the most valuable of all lures to the angler. In the first chapter of this volume it was mentioned that at least twelve pounds weight of trout might be captured almost any day during the angling season, and for three months it is by fly alone that this must be accomplished. There are few anglers aware of the service the artificial fly is capable of rendering if properly used. James Baillie, whom we have already introduced to the reader, but whose hazel rod and string tied to the top of it are familiar to all those in the habit of frequenting Leader or Gala, maintains himself and family from March to November by fly-fishing exclusively. We believe this notable person kills on an average from twelve to fourteen pounds at each excursion, and, being in delicate health, he only fishes for four or five hours a-day. If our amateur friends had to make their living by fly-fishing, there are few of them we would care for dining with often.

Besides being the most attractive and valuable,

artificial fly-fishing is the most difficult branch of the angler's art, and this is another reason of the preference accorded to it, since there is more merit, and therefore more pleasure, in excelling in what is difficult. An opinion, however, has of late years been gaining ground, that worm-fishing in a clear water is more difficult than fly-fishing. This opinion has been supported by Mr. Stoddart, who says :—" It may perhaps startle some, and those no novices in the art, when I declare, and offer more-over to prove, that worm-fishing for trout requires essentially more address and experience, as well as a better knowledge of the habits and instincts of the trout, than fly-fishing. I do not, be it observed, refer to the practice of this branch of the art as it is followed in hill-burns and petty rivulets, neither do I allude to it as pursued after heavy rains in flooded and discoloured waters ; my affirmation bears solely upon its practice as carried on during the summer months in the southern districts of Scot-land, when the rivers are clear and low, and the skies bright and warm."*

This is an opinion from which we entirely dis-sent, and though Mr. Stoddart offers to prove his assertion, he does not attempt doing so. That there are fewer worm-fishers who meet with success when the waters are clear, than there are fly-fishers who meet with success when the waters are coloured, we admit. But between fly-fishing when the waters

* Stoddart's *Angler's Companion*, chapter vi. page 106.

are swollen after rain, or as it is practised among unwary fish in Highland streams, and fly-fishing in our much-fished southern streams when the waters are clear, we draw the same distinction as Mr. Stoddart does between worm-fishing in a coloured water and a clear one ; and the number of fly-fishers who meet with success under the circumstances just mentioned is exceedingly limited.

In trouting with the minnow, worm, or natural fly, the angler has the real fish, worm, or insect, with which to entice the trout, but in fly-fishing he has, by means of a few feathers, to deceive the wary keen-sighted fish, and make it believe that his imitation is a natural fly either alive or dead. Any one will at once see that this is the more difficult, and that to prevail upon a trout to seize a reality does not afford room for the exercise of so much skill as to prevail upon the same trout to seize an imitation. Hence fly-fishing, in the same condition of water, requires more address than angling with the worm, or any other known method ; and consequently, fly-fishing in a clear low water is, beyond comparison, the most difficult of all the branches of the angler's art, and should therefore rank highest as sport.

This, however, is not an art that can be learned in a day, or so easily as some seem to imagine. A beginner becomes enamoured of fly-fishing. For six weeks he grinds at Walton and all the other authorities upon the subject, and having equipped himself with all the paraphernalia for waging a war of extermination upon the finny tribe, he rolls his hat round with cast after cast of flies, which bear a far greater resemblance to humble-bees than river insects; and thus accoutred sets out to put his acquired information in practice. Arrived at the river-side he finds his mistake: if the water be swollen, and of the dark porter colour so celebrated among anglers, he may be rewarded with the capture of a few trout; but if it be clear, he plies his lure to the terror and alarm of almost every trout in the water, and returns, if not with an empty basket, at least with a very light one, to confirm the prevailing opinion that it is of no use fishing when the water is clear. If this opinion were correct, it would limit the time when angling could be successfully prac- tised to a few weeks in the season, and sometimes to a few days; but fortunately for the angler it is not correct, being merely the natural result of a mode of angling which ignores the habits and instincts of the trout. Trout are just as much inclined to feed when the waters are clear as when they are coloured. In a clear water they may be seen rising in immense numbers at the natural insect, showing that they are not inclined to starve in these circumstances.

When the water is of a dark colour, it conceals the angler from view, and disguises his tackle, and so he meets with fair sport. If the body of water, though clear, is sufficiently large to conceal him from the sight of the trout, as in Tweed, Tay, and other first-class streams, he may still meet with tolerable

success. But in all our small rivers and waters,
when they are low and clear, not one angler out of
twenty meets with much sport, and the reason of it
is, because the clearness of the water either allows
the trout to see him, or enables them to detect the
artificial nature of his lure ; and to meet these difficulties as far as possible, is the great object to be
aimed at in fly-fishing.

The great error of fly-fishing, as usually practised,
and as recommended to be practised by books, is
that the angler fishes down stream, whereas he should
fish up.

We believe we are not beyond the mark in
stating that ninety-nine anglers out of a hundred fish
down with the artificial fly ; they never think of
fishing in any other way, and never dream of attri-
buting their want of success to it. Yet we are
prepared to prove, both in theory and practice, that
this is the greatest reason of their want of success
in clear waters. In all our angling excursions we
have only met one or two amateurs, and a few profes-
sionals, who fished up stream with the fly, and used
it in a really artistic manner. If the wind is blowing up, anglers will occasionally fish up the pools
—(as for fishing up a strong stream they never
think of it)—but even then they do not do it properly, and meet with little better success than if they
had followed their usual method. They will also,
if going to some place up a river, walk up, not fish
up to it—their plan being to go to the top of a pool,

and then fish it down, never casting their line above them at all.

We shall now mention in detail the advantages. of fishing up, in order to show its superiority over the old method.

The first and greatest advantage is, that the angler is unseen by the trout.   Trout, as is well known, keep their heads up stream ; they cannot remain stationary in any other position.   This being the case, they see objects above and on both sides of, them, but cannot discern anything behind them, so that the angler fishing down will be seen by them twenty yards off, whereas the angler fishing up will be unseen, although he be but a few yards in their rear.   The advantages of this it is impossible to over-estimate.   No creatures are more easily scared than trout ; if they see any object moving on the river's bank, they run into deep water, or beneath banks and stones, from which they will not stir for some time.   A bird flying across the water, or the shadow of a rod, will sometimes alarm them ; and nothing connected with angling is more certain than this, that if the trout see the angler, they will not take his lure.   He may ply his minnow in the most captivating manner, may throw his worm with con-summate skill, or make his flies light softly as a gossamer—all will be unavailing if he is seen by his intended victim.

The next advantage of fishing up we shall notice, is the much greater probability of hooking a trout when it rises. In angling down stream, if a trout rises and the angler strikes, he runs a great risk of pulling the flies straight out of its mouth ; whereas, in fishing up, its back is to him, and he has every chance of bringing the hook into contact with its jaws. This, although it may not seem of great importance to the uninitiated, tells considerably when the contents of the basket come to be examined at the close of the day's sport ; indeed no angler would believe the difference unless he himself proved it.

Another advantage of fishing up is, that it does not disturb the water so much. Let us suppose the angler is fishing down a fine pool. He, of course, commences at the top, the place where the best trout, and those most inclined to feed, invariably lie. After a few casts he hooks one, which immediately runs down, and by its vagaries, leaping in the air, and plunging in all directions, alarms all its neighbours, and it is ten to one if he gets another rise in that pool. Fishing up saves all this. The angler commences at the foot, and when he hooks a trout, pulls it down, and the remaining portions of the pool are undisturbed. This is a matter of great importance, and we have frequently, in small streams, taken a dozen trout out of a pool, from which, had we been fishing down, we could not possibly have got more than two or three.

The last advantage of fishing up is, that by it the angler can much better adapt the motions of his flies to those of the natural insect. And here it may be mentioned as a rule, that the nearer the motions of the artificial flies resemble those of the natural ones under similar circumstances, the greater will be the prospects of success. Whatever trout take the artificial fly for, it is obvious they are much more likely to be deceived by a natural than by an unnatural motion.

No method of angling can imitate the hovering flight of an insect along the surface of the water, now just touching it, then flying a short distance, and so on ; and for the angler to attempt by any motion of his hand to give his flies a living appearance is mere absurdity. The only moment when trout may mistake the angler's fly for a real one in its flight, is the moment it first touches the water ; and in this respect fishing down possesses equal advantages with fishing up. But this is the only respect, and in order to illustrate this, we shall give a brief description of fly-fishing as usually practised down stream.

The angler, then, we shall suppose, commences operations at the head of a pool or stream, and, throwing his flies as far as he can across from where he is standing, raises his rod and brings them gradually to his own side of the water. He then steps down a yard or two, repeats the process, and so on. Having dismissed the idea that the angler can imitate the flight of a living fly along the surface of the water, we must suppose that trout take the artificial fly for a dead one, or one which has fairly got into the stream and lost all power of re-sisting. A feeble motion of the wings or legs would be the only attempt at escape which a live fly in such a case could make. What then must be the astonishment of the trout, when they see the tiny. insect which they are accustomed to seize as it is carried by the current towards them, crossing the stream with the strength and agility of an otter? Is it not much more natural to throw the flies up and let them come gently down as any real insect would do?

In addition to drawing their flies across the stream, some anglers practise what is called playing their flies, which is done by a jerking motion of the wrist, which imparts a similar motion to the fly. Their object in doing this is to create an appearance of life, and thus render their flies more attractive. An appearance of life is certainly a great temptation to a trout, but it may be much better accomplished by dressing the flies of soft materials, which the water can agitate, and thus create a natural motion of the legs or wings of the fly, than by dragging them by jumps of a foot at a time across and up a roaring stream. Trout are not accustomed to see small insects making such gigantic efforts at escape, and therefore it is calculated to awaken their suspicions.

We believe that all fly-fishers fishing down must have noticed, that apart from the moment of alight-ing, they get more rises for the first few yards of their flies' course than in the whole of the remainder; and that when their flies fairly breast the stream they seldom get a rise at all. The reason of this is clear :—for the first few feet after the angler throws his flies across the stream they swim with the current; the moment, however, he begins to describe his semicircle across the water, they present an unnatural appearance, which the trout view with distrust. Experienced fly-fishers, following the old method, who have observed this, and are aware of the great importance of the moment their flies alight, cast very frequently, only allowing their flies to float down a few feet, when they throw again. We have seen some Tweedside adepts fill capital baskets in this way; but, as we have before stated, it will only succeed when the water is coloured, or when there is a body of clear water sufficiently large to conceal the angler from view; and even then he may have much better sport by fishing up. The angler drawing his flies across and up stream will catch trout, and this is the strongest evidence that trout are not such profound philosophers as the notions of some would lead us to suppose. But though he does catch trout, they are in general the very smallest. Indeed, the advantages of fishing up are in nothing more apparent than in the superior size of the trout captured. We believe they will average nearly double the size of those caught with the same flies fishing down, and though generally not so large as those taken with the worm, they are not much

F

behind them, and we almost invariably kill a few larger trout in a river with the fly than with the worm.

Though our remarks in this chapter have principally reference to angling in small rivers, where fishing up is *essential* to success, the same arguments hold good in every size or colour of water in a less degree, as even though the trout cannot see the angler, the other advantages which we have mentioned are still in his favour.

If we were fishing a large river when it was dark-coloured, and required to wade deep, we should fish down, because the fatigue of wading up would, under such circumstances, become a serious drawback. In such a case we fish in the following manner :— Throwing our flies, partly up and partly across from where. we are standing, we allow them to swim down a yard or two, when we cast again, never allowing them to go below that part of the stream opposite us. But though the angler gets over the ground as quickly this way, and casts as often, as if he were fishing up, yet he has not the same chance, because if a trout catches sight of his flies just as he is lifting them, their sudden abstraction may deter it from taking them on their again alighting ; whereas in fishing up the angler casts a yard or two further up every time, so that every trout may see his flies at the moment they alight.

The reader must not suppose that fishing up is all that is necessary for success ; on the contrary, the angler may throw his flies up stream, and know less of the art of fly-fishing, and catch fewer trout, than his neighbour who is fishing down. The mere fact of an angler throwing his flies up stream is no proof that he is a fly-fisher. Of those who fish down stream some catch more and some less, and in like manner with those fishing up, one may catch three times as many as another, depending upon the particular method they adopt ; and unless the reader pays *strict* attention to the details which will be mentioned subsequently, we are afraid he will not derive much benefit. Fishing up is *much more* difficult than fishing down, requiring more practice, and a better acquaintance with the habits of the trout ; and we believe that a mere novice would, in a large water, catch more trout by fishing down than up, because the latter *requires more nicety* in casting. But to attain anything like eminence in fly-fishing, the angler *must* fish up, and all beginners should *persevere* in it, even though they meet with little success at first, and they will be amply rewarded for their trouble.

The only circumstance in which fishing down has the advantage of fishing up, is when the water is so dark or deep that the fish would not see, or if they did see, would not have time to seize the flies, unless they moved at a slower rate than the stream. We think that this rarely applies to angling for river trout, as when inclined to feed upon flies they are generally on the outlook for them, but it does apply to salmon and sea-trout fishing. Both these fish lie in strong deep water, and as they are not accustomed to feed upon flies, they are not on the outlook for them ; so that if the salmon-fisher were to throw his flies up stream, they would come down at such a rate that the salmon would never see them. Besides which, it is obvious that whatever salmon take the angler's fly for, they cannot take it for anything they have seen before, and therefore there is no reason for supposing they can detect anything unnatural in its motion.

We have devoted this chapter principally to the errors of fly-fishing as generally practised, and we hope we have succeeded in convincing the reader of the truth of our observations ; but as we have frequently endeavoured in vain by *viva voce* demonstration to persuade anglers to fish up, we have no doubt numbers will adhere to their own way. As no amount of mere argument will convince such, we offer to find two anglers, who, in a water suitable for showing the superiority of fishing up, will be more successful than any three anglers fishing down after the ordinary method.

We have just given the same reasons for fishing up stream as in our first edition, because upon this point there can be nothing new; and are as ready as ever to find anglers who are prepared to do battle in their behalf, on the terms just stated ; but while one or two have come forward to dispute the theory, none have accepted our challenge and come forward to dispute the practice. One reviewer—the only objector we recollect of who gives a reason—says, "that so long as streams run down, carrying the food of the fish with them, so long should anglers fish down." This seems said purely for the sake of appearing to give a reason; and while his premises are undeniably correct, we entirely dissent from his conclusions. Streams certainly run down and carry the food of the trout with them, but along with that food they do not carry an apparition in the shape of an angler with rod and line upon the bank; and as nothing will familiarise them to such an apparition, we draw the conclusion that that apparition had better keep out of sight and fish up stream. Moreover, the fact that the natural food floats down is anything but a reason that the artificial lure in imitation of that food should be pulled up.

We must confess, however, that fishing up stream with fly has not been adopted by a large portion of the angling community, and that for various reasons. In spite of the strong manner in which we cautioned our readers about the difficulties of fishing up stream, numbers who read the arguments for it, and were struck with the soundness of the theory, thought they saw at a glance the cause of their previous want of success, and that in future the result would be different. Having equipped themselves à la *Practical Angler*, and even taken a copy of that excellent work in their pockets, they started with high hopes on their new career, but the

result was not different, and after one or two trials
with no better success, not a few have condemned
fishing up stream as erroneous and ourselves as
impostors ; though we imagine the fault lies with
themselves. We have met anglers fishing down
stream—and this is no supposititious case, but one
which we have seen over and over again—with a
copy of this volume in their pockets, who complained that they had got everything herein recommended and were getting no sport. On pointing out
to them that there was one important mistake they
were committing, in fishing down stream instead of
up, they stated that when they came to a pool they
fished it up—that is to say, they first walked down
the pool and showed themselves to the trout, and
then commenced to fish for them.

> "The trout within yon wimplin' burn,
>   Glides swift, a silver dart ;
> And safe beneath the shady thorn,
>   Defies the angler's art."

John Younger objects to this as incorrect, but
we rather think that Burns is right, and the angler
wrong ; as it is evident the poet alludes to a trout
that has caught sight of the angler, and safe he is,
at least *pro tem.*, as our pupils who first frighten the
fish by walking down a pool-side, and then fish up
it, will find to their cost.

Others object to fishing up stream, as requiring
too frequent casting, being too fatiguing, and because
they have been accustomed to fish down, and would

prefer fishing in that way, even though they do not catch so many trout. If any angler prefers catching five pounds weight of trout fishing down stream, to ten pounds weight fishing up, we may wonder at his taste, but it is no concern of ours. Our duty is to point out how most trout can be captured in a given time; and that is by fishing up stream, and such is now the method adopted by all the best fly-fishers of the day.

Those anglers who have adopted fishing up stream are principally those who were adepts in the old system, and who were possessed of all the nicety in casting, and other knowledge so essential to successful up-stream fishing.

The art of fly-fishing—or fishing of any kind—may be summed up in knowing what to fish with, and how, when, and where to fish. We have rather transposed the arrangement, and taken part of the second division first, because it is necessary to establish whether the angler should fish up or down, before considering what he is to fish with, different tackle being necessary for the former method. In the subsequent chapters we shall return to the proper arrangement, and shall complete in its proper place the division already half finished.

CHAPTER V.

HE practice of using artificial flies has undoubtedly had its origin in the necessity
for imitating insects, which cannot be
used in their natural state. From the
first rude attempt at fly-making of some ingenious angler, the art has gone on progress-
ing, the number of imitations always increasing, and the prevalent opinion always being
that, in order to fish successfully, the angler
must use an imitation of one or other of the natural
insects on the water at the time. In spite of the
exertions of Mr. Wilson and Mr. Stoddart to incul-
cate an opposite theory, this opinion is still held by
the great majority of anglers in Scotland, while in
England it is all but universal.

Anglers holding these views rejoice in the possession of as many different varieties of flies as
would stock a fishing-book, all of which they consider imitations of so many real insects, and classify
under the heads of the different months when these
appear. They have a fly for the morning, another

for noon, and another for the evening of every day in the year, and spend a great deal of time in taking off one fly, because it is a shade too dark, and a second because it is a shade too light, and a third to give place to the imitation of some insect which has just made its appearance on the water.

During the summer months it is supposed that the varieties of insects are reckoned by the thousand, and we have seen several dozens of different kinds on the water at one time, all of which are greedily devoured by the trout. Those anglers who think trout will take no fly unless it is an exact imitation of some one of the immense number of flies they are feeding on, must suppose that they know to a shade the colour of every fly on the water, and can detect the least deviation from it—an amount of entomological knowledge that would put to shame the angler himself, and a good many naturalists to boot. This opinion arises from the supposition that trout will not take anything readily unless they are accustomed to feed upon it, and consequently that they will not take a fly unless it has been on the water sufficiently long to allow them to become acquainted with it. Nothing can be more erroneous than this. Trout will take worms and grubs which they have never seen before. They will also take parr-tail readily, and they can never have seen it before; and in like manner with other things; and there is no reason why fly should be an exception.

We do not think it at all likely that trout can

see the colour of a fly very distinctly. The worst light of all for seeing its colour is when it is placed between you and the sky, as the trout see it. And when the fly is rolled round by every current, and sometimes seen through the medium of a few feet of running water, the idea that they can detect its colour to a shade is highly improbable. Even granting they could, there is no reason for supposing they would reject it on that account. Flies of the same kind differ so much in colour that we could show the reader a May-fly almost black, and a May-fly almost yellow, and of all the intermediate shades.

It is singular inconsistency, that anglers scrupulously exact about a shade of colour draw their flies across and up stream in a way in which no natural insect was ever seen moving, as if a trout could not detect an alteration in the motion much more easily than a deviation in the colour of a fly.

The argument brought by anglers in support of these views is, that having fished unsuccessfully all the morning, they changed their flies and had good sport, or that when they were getting nothing they met with some celebrated local angler, who gave them the fly peculiar to the district, after which they met with success. We think that on most of these occasions the trout take better, not because the new fly is more to their liking, but because as the day advances they are more inclined to feed. We have frequently proved this by re-changing to our flies which at first proved unsuccessful, and

have almost invariably found they were as killing
as their predecessors. Other causes also operate.
The thread of gut on which the fly is dressed is of
more importance than the fly itself ; and those professional anglers who haunt most southern streams,
and whose " fail-me-never" is the only fly suitable
for the water—because they expect to be well paid
for it—take care to have their flies dressed on fine
gut.

Such a difference does the gut make, that if
an angler will take two threads of gut of the same
thickness, but one of a glossy white colour, and the
other clear and transparent, and dress two flies upon
them exactly alike, the fly dressed on the clear gut
will kill two trout for one which the fly dressed on
the white gut will. The shape of the fly will also
make a great difference, and really practical anglers,
such as all those who make their living by it are,
do not put a third of the feathers on their flies that
some town-made ones have.

We have frequently got flies, which, we were
assured, were exact imitations of some fly on the
water at the time, and which the donors were certain would kill more trout than any other, but on
trying them we did not find them so deadly as those
we were using ; and they killed quite as well, and
sometimes better, two months before the natural fly
came on the water, or two months after it was gone.
We think it just possible that when a large fly,
such as the green drake, remains a long time on the

water, trout may recognise it, and when the waters are dark coloured and there is a strong breeze of wind, take an imitation of it more readily than any other. But in our own experience we have never found this to be the case ; and though we have frequently tried this fly—so celebrated on English streams—we have never found it nearly so deadly as our usual flies, even when the water was coloured ; and in clear water it failed entirely, as all large 'flies will, for the obvious reason that their size enables the trout to detect their artificial nature. Furthermore, we have killed more trout with this imitation in the month of May, before the real insects had made their appearance, than in June, when the water was swarming with them, which we ascribe to the circumstance that trout will take a larger fly in May than in June.

This opinion would not have been maintained so long, but that there is at first sight a degree of plausibility about it, and that it does not to any great extent interfere with the successful practice of fly-fishing. What is meant for an imitation of a particular fly may occasionally do good service ; not because the trout see any resemblance between it and the fly it is intended to imitate, but because, if the size and colour are suitable, it will just kill as well as any other. And we believe the angler who has a different fly for every day in the season will kill nearly as many trout as the angler who adheres to three or four varieties the whole season through ;

but he is proceeding upon an erroneous principle, and losing both labour and time.

That trout sometimes take more readily flies of one colour than another is certain, and the reason of their doing so affords room for a great deal of ingenious speculation, but is exceedingly difficult to ascertain satisfactorily. We think that to some extent a certain colour is more deadly, because it is more readily seen. In clear waters we have rarely found a black fly surpassed by any other, and in such circumstances a black fly is very easily seen. In dark waters a yellow-bodied fly, or one of dingy white colour, takes readily, being easily seen. And on Tweedside, in the month of July, just after sunset, a bright yellow fly is held in great repute, and such is more likely to attract attention than any other. Mere caprice, however, and love of variety, may be the main reasons why the trout prefer one colour to another.

A rule to be guided by on this point is of little use, as the angler can always regulate the colour of his flies by practice ; and in practice it has been proved beyond doubt, that a black, brown, red, and dun-coloured fly, used together, and varied in size according to circumstances, will at any time kill as well, and even better, than the most elaborate collection arranged for every month in the year. If trout are at all inclined to rise, one or other of the above will be found inviting. It is quite clear that whatever the angler's opinion with regard to flies

may be—whether he believes that he must have an
imitation of some insect on the water at the time,
that he must have a fly of the same colour as the
majority of those on the water, or with ourselves
holds neither of these opinions ; if he has four flies
such as those mentioned above, he cannot be very
far off the mark, as these comprise all the leading
colours of which insects generally are.

The opinion that it is necessary to imitate the
particular fly on the water at the time has recently
received the weight of Mr. Francis Francis' support,
who in advocating what may be called the English
theory gives a sort of side-wipe to Scotch anglers—the
drift of his remarks being, that though a small assort-
ment of flies may do well enough in Scotch streams
where little fishing goes on and anglers count their
takes by the dozen, it will not answer in the much-
fished streams on the other side of the Border, where
anglers count their takes by the brace. If Mr.
Francis' views as to an exact imitation being necessary
in English streams be correct, which we very much
doubt, he will require to find some other reason for
its being unnecessary in Scotland than this. In com-
paring the severity of the fishing in Scotch and
English streams it must be borne in mind that the
former are, as a rule, open to the public, and that the
latter, as a rule, are preserved and fished only by a
favoured few. If Mr. Francis will point out any
stream in England, in which he thinks it worth
while to throw a fly for trout, that is more and better
fished than Tweed and its tributaries, we shall be

very much surprised. And on behalf of Scotch anglers we repudiate with scorn the bare idea that it requires less skill to catch a Scotch trout than an English one, or that the former in any way receives an inferior education as regards flies, etc, to his English brother.   In fact, we believe that in the before-mentioned streams the education of the inhabitants is as superior to that of the inhabitants of English streams as the education of the people of the one country is admitted to be to that of the other ; and supposing the most accomplished believer in the English theory— aye, even Mr. Francis himself—engaged on a mile of Tweed along with twenty or thirty Galashiels weavers (by no means an unusual number), we question if his basket at the finish would illustrate very strongly the superiority of his theory and practice.   We have met English anglers even in Scotland counting their takes by the brace, and not in much danger of going wrong in their reckoning either.   Having relieved our feelings of this protest on behalf of Scotch anglers and Scotch trout, we must now consider what it is necessary to imitate, or what do trout take, or rather mistake, the artificial fly for.   As before stated, we believe that, deceived by an appearance of life, they take it for what it is intended to imitate— a fly or some other aquatic insect.   In proof of this, artificial flies are not of much use unless the trout are at the time feeding on the natural insect.   And an artificial fly will kill twenty trout for one which the feathers composing it, rolled round the hook without regard to shape, will.   Nay, more; a neatly-made, natural-looking fly will, where trout are shy, kill three trout for one which a clumsy fly will; and a fly with the exposed part of the hook taken off will raise more trout than a fly with the same left on. In the first case, the trout see no resemblance in form to anything they are accustomed to feed upon, and, unless very hungry, decline to seize it. In the second case, the resemblance to nature not being so complete in the one fly as in the other, fewer trout are deceived by it. The third case shows that trout can detect that a hook is an unnatural appendage.

The great point, then, in fly-dressing, is to make the artificial fly resemble the natural insect in shape, and the great characteristic of all river insects is extreme lightness and neatness of form. Our great objection to the flies in common use is, that they are much too bushy; so much so, that there are few flies to be got in the tackle-shops which we could use with any degree of confidence in clear water. Every possible advantage is in favour of a lightly-dressed fly; it is more like a natural insect; it falls lighter on the water, and every angler knows the importance of making his fly fall gently, and there being less material about it, the artificial nature of that material is not so easily detected; and also, as the hook is not so much covered with feathers, there is a much better chance of hooking a trout when it rises. We wish to impress very strongly upon the reader the *necessity of avoiding bulky flies.*

The artificial flies in commom use may be divided into two classes. There is first the winged fly, which alone, properly speaking, merits the appellation; and there is the palmer hackle or spider, by which last name we mean to call it, believing that if it resembles anything in the insect tribe, it is a spider. As a means of capturing trout, we rank them higher than the winged imitations. When trout are taking, winged flies will answer very well; and sometimes, but very rarely, we have found them more killing than spiders. But in the summer months, when trout are well fed and become lazy, or where they are much fished for, and become shy, we have found spiders much more deadly than the most tempting winged fly that can be made. Nor is it necessary to go very much out of the way to seek a reason for this : the hook is better concealed, and if made of sufficiently soft materials, the water agitates the feathers, and gives them a life-like appearance, which has a wonderful effect, and is of itself a sufficient reason for trout preferring them, without supposing, as some do, that spiders are greater rarities than flies, with a variety of other fine-spun theories.

By universal consent, feathers seem to have been fixed upon as the most suitable materials for imitating flies. Some years ago gutta percha wings were tried, but in every respect they are inferior. The selection of proper feathers requires some care ; they should always be taken from the birds when in their

G

full, plumage, which is usually about Christmas. Among those considered most necessary are hackles, which are usually taken from the neck of the common cock. It is very difficult to procure them of the right colour, and still more so to procure them of the right shape. In a proper hackle the fibres should be longest at the root end, and taper gradually towards the point. It is not one cock out of twenty whose hackles merit the attention of the fly-dresser.

The hackle generally plays a very conspicuous part in the construction of trouting flies. The spider or hackle fly is made of it entirely, and in other flies it is used to imitate the legs of the insect. We, however, think the cock-hackle by no means deserving of so much attention as is bestowed upon it, being too stiff and wiry to represent the legs of an insect, and we prefer hen-hackles, or still better, the small feathers taken from the neck or outside of the wings of a variety of small birds. But these latter are not always to be had of the colour wanted, and cock-hackles are very convenient to fall back upon, but should be selected as soft in the fibre as possible. Amongst those most serviceable to the angler are the small feathers taken from the outside of the wings, as also from the neck and shoulders of the following birds :—The starling, landrail, dotterel, mavis, grey plover, golden plover, partridge, and grouse. Of the foregoing, we consider the feathers taken from the cock starling the most valuable of all to the angler. They have a rich glossy black, which no other feathers possess, and we always use them in place of the black cock-hackle. Next to them we rank the feathers of a reddish-brown colour taken from the outside of the wing of the landrail, the only feathers which take the place of the red cock-hackle; and as it is impossible to get any quantity of these sufficiently small, we frequently find it necessary to have recourse to red hackles.

The feathers of the dotterel are also held in high esteem, but all those just mentioned may with advantage be substituted for the hackle in the formation of all trouting flies and spiders. Their superiority consists in their much greater resemblance to the legs of an insect, and their extreme softness. So soft are they, that when a spider is made of one of them and placed in the water, the least motion will agitate and impart a singularly life-like appearance to it, whereas it would have no effect upon a cock-hackle. Spiders dressed of very soft feathers are more suitable for fishing up than for fishing down, as, if drawn against the stream, it runs the fibres alongside of the hook, and all resemblance to an insect is destroyed.

Killing spiders may be made of all the feathers we have mentioned, but the three following are all we consider necessary :—

1st. The Black Spider.—This is made of the small feather of the cock starling, dressed with *Re* *or orange well waxed* brown silk, and is, upon the whole, the most killing imitation we know. We were first shown it by

James Baillie, and have never been without one on
our line ever since.

2d. The Red Spider should be made of the small
feather taken from the outside of the wing of the
landrail, dressed with yellow silk, and is deserving
of a very high rank, particularly in coloured water.

3d. The Dun Spider.—This should be made of
the small soft dun or ash-coloured feather, taken
from the outside of the wing of the dotterel. This
bird is unfortunately very scarce ; but a small
feather may be taken from the inside of the wing
of the starling, which will make an excellent substitute.

The only objection to spiders is, that the feathers
are so soft that the trout's teeth break them off, and
after catching a dozen or two of trout, little is left
of them but the bare dressing, rendering it necessary
for the angler to change them ; and if the trout are
taking.readily, this has to be repeated two or three
times a-day.   For this reason we always use winged
flies, when they take equally well, which, if well
dressed, will last a whole day or ˙even two.   For
making flies, in addition to the feathers before mentioned, the wings of the following birds are necessary :—Corn-bunting, lark, chaffinch, woodcock, and
landrail.   These are used to make the wings of the
flies, but dubbing of some sort is also necessary to
form the body, and for this purpose there is nothing
better than the fur of a hare's ear, or, as it is usually
called in Scotland, "hare-lug."   A good hare-lug

will make body for five or six gross of flies of all
colours, from dingy white to dark black, but the
mixed dark fur is the best. The fur of the water-
rat is also serviceable to the fly-dresser, and is peculiarly suitable for small flies. The three following
are the winged flies to which we are most partial :—

1st. A woodcock wing with a single turn of a
red hackle, or landrail feather, dressed with yellow
silk, freely exposed on the body. For fishing in
dark-coloured waters, this fly may be dressed with
scarlet thread.

2d. A hare-lug body, with a corn-bunting or
chaffinch wing. A woodcock wing may also be put in
the same body, but should be made of the small light-
coloured feather taken from the inside of the wing.

3d. The same wing as the last fly, with a single
turn of a soft black hen-hackle, or small feather
taken from the shoulder of the starling, dressed
with dark-coloured silk. *purple* .

An immense number of killing flies may be
made by varying the wings and body, but nothing
is gained by extending the number beyond those
just mentioned, and we do not believe six more killing imitations can be manufactured. We have fished
with flies of all kinds, and got flies from several of
the best anglers, both amateur and professional, but
have never found anything superior to these, and
we can recommend them with great confidence.

For fly-dressing, in addition to the feathers, etc.,
just mentioned, a number of miscellaneous articles

are necessary—namely, brass nippers for putting on
small feathers or hackles ; a pair of fine scissors,
curved at the points ; a needle for dividing wings
and raising dubbing ; silk of all colours, the thinner
the better, as it makes the firmer dressing ; shoe-
maker's wax, and a mixture of resin and burgundy
pitch, to be used when the colour of the silk is intended to be shown on the fly ; hooks of all sizes,
the bend to be particularly attended to. The size
of hook should always bear some proportion to the
size of fly, but the exact size of hook that will be
most killing with a fly of a certain size is exceedingly difficult to determine. Some of the shop flies
are dressed upon hooks so small, and rolled round
with so much dubbing and hackle, that we would
consider their chances of hooking one trout out of
ten rises exceedingly problematical. We have frequently fished with a very small fly, say No. 15,
and a larger fly, say No. 12, of the same kind, and
found that though the smaller fly raised twice the
number, it did not secure so many as the larger one.
We have also tried dressing two flies of the same
kind and size, one on a No. 14, and the other on a
No. 12 hook. The No. 12 was of course very much
exposed, notwithstanding which it did most execution. This should be done very cautiously ; but
by having hooks made a size thinner in the wire,
they may be used one size larger with perfect safety.
We have endeavoured to indicate the proper size of
hook in a subsequent illustration.

Great care should be taken to select the finest and longest threads of gut for dressing flies on. When the waters are clear, fine gut is quite as necessary as good flies ; the finest gut, however lightly thrown, will sometimes alarm the trout.

Dressing a spider is a much simpler operation than dressing a fly, and therefore it is better to begin with it. Having selected a thread of gut and a hook, the next thing is to choose a feather, which, to make a neat spider, must be so proportioned to the size of the hook, that the legs of the spider, when dressed, will be about the length of the hook. Before commencing, bite the end of the gut between your teeth ; this flattens and makes it broader in the point, which prevents it slipping ; a thing very liable to occur with small flies. Next, take the hook firmly between the forefinger and thumb of your left hand, lay the gut along its shank, and with a well-waxed silk thread, commencing about the centre of the hook, whip it and the gut firmly together, till you come to the end of the shank, where form the head by a few turns of the thread. This done, take the feather, and laying it on with the root end towards the bend of the hook, wrap the silk three or four times round it, and then cut off the root end.

What remains to be done is the most critical part of the whole operation ; still holding the hook between the forefinger and thumb of your left hand, take the thread, lay it along the centre of the inside

of the feather, and with the forefinger and thumb
of your right hand twirl them round together till
the feather is rolled round the thread ; and in this
state wrap it round the hook, taking care that a
sufficient number of the fibres stick out to represent
the legs ; to effect this it will sometimes be necessary to raise the fibres with a needle during the
operation. Having carried the feather and thread
down to where you commenced, wrap the silk three
or four times round the end of the feather, and if
there is any left cut it off, and finish with a succession of hitch-knots, or the common whip-fastening.
If the legs of the spider when dressed are too long,
there is no remedy for it ; cutting injures rather
than improves them. This is a very rough and
simple mode of dressing a spider, and does not
make it so neat as if the feather were put on by a
pair of nippers, but it is more natural-looking, and
much more durable, as the feather is fastened on by
the thread the whole way down.

A fly is more difficult to dress neatly than a
spider. Having selected the gut and hook, take
the feather of which you intend to make the wings,
and stripping off as much as you require, fold it up,
taking care that the lightest coloured side of the
feather is outside, and lay it beside the other
materials. It is quite common in fishing-tackle
shops to see the wings put on singly—that is to
say, consisting of merely one fold of the feather.
This makes a beautiful fly out of the water, but

when once wet, is of little further use, as the fibres run together, and form a mere thread. The wings should consist of several folds of the feather, as then they keep their original shape, wetting improving rather than injuring their appearance.

In dressing a fly, commence in the same manner as in dressing a spider, carrying the thread up to within three or four turns of the end of the shank; then take the feathers, of which you are to form the wings, firmly between the forefinger and thumb of your right hand, lay it to the bare end of the shank, whip the thread firmly round it two or three times, and then cut off the root end of the feather as close as possible. To put on the wings neatly, and make them lie properly, is the most difficult part of fly-making, and care must be taken to lay them on so that, when fastened, they will be the proper length, as it does not do to cut them. The wings being now fastened on, but in a whole, divide them, and passing the silk between them, bring it up crossways.

So far, the dressing of all flies is alike, but the remainder of the operation depends upon whether the fly is to be dressed with a hackle or dubbing.

If it is to be made with dubbing, all that remains to be done is to take a little of it, and applying it to the silk with the forefinger and thumb of the right hand, twist them both together till the dubbing is thoroughly rolled round the silk; and in that state wrap it round the hook till the body of the fly is made, when finish as usual; then with a needle raise a few of the hairs of the dubbing, close to the head of the fly, to give it a feathery appearance.

If the fly is to be dressed with a feather or hackle, after having put on the wings lay the hackle on as in dressing a spider, with the root end towards the bend of the hook; fasten it on and cut off the root end. Next take hold of the end of the hackle with your brass nippers, and turn it once or twice round the hook as close under the wings as possible; then wrap the silk three or four times round it to make it secure, cut off the remainder, and carry the thread by itself down to where you intend finishing. In a large fly it will be an improvement to put on a little dubbing of the same colour as the body of the fly, after having put on the hackle. The most expeditious way of dressing flies is to dress say a dozen of one kind at a time, selecting and arranging all the materials necessary before commencing.

The following illustration shows what appearance the flies should present when finished.

The first of the accompanying flies is a spider, the second a fly dressed with dubbing, and the third a fly dressed with a hackle. The reader will observe that these flies are very light in the make; that there is not more dubbing than cover the thread; that the hackle is put on very sparingly; and that the dressing is not carried far down the hook. Anglers accustomed to shop-made flies may think this is carried to an extreme, but we have met

anglers using flies with sufficient dubbing on them,
to have made body for half-a-dozen flies, each fly
more killing than the original ; and as a last advice
upon flies, we advise all anglers to use them very
light. The spider is made rather more bushy than
is advisable at first, as the trout's teeth would otherwise tear it away too fast. After capturing a dozen
trout it will be spare enough.

It is exceedingly difficult by means of written
instructions to make fly-dressing intelligible to the
reader ; a few lessons would do more than a whole
volume of instructions.

It is very difficult to dress flies neatly, and
unless anglers have plenty of time to devote to it,
they would act wisely in purchasing their flies from
professional dressers, who will make them to any
pattern ; but anglers should see that they *are* dressed
to pattern. Since the first edition was published, our
friends have shown us flies which they bought as
being the kind we recommended, and as being tied
on fine gut, but which were the identical bushy flies
which we have devoted so many pages to warn
anglers against ; and as for the gut, it was so thick
and coarse as to preclude the possibility of success,
in anything like fine fishing. All the knowledge of

the habits of the trout, all the skill, all the energy, possessed by the most accomplished angler are merely thrown away in the use of such tackle ; no angler, not even James Baillie, could fill even a small basket in clear water with such tackle. We have given illustrations for the very purpose that anglers may compare their flies with them, but it is impossible that fishing-tackle makers can take the care necessary to make proper flies, dress them on the finest gut, and sell them at the present price.

Several flies are always used together, and the method of joining them, or, as it is usually called, making up the fly-cast, is a point of some importance. The two things most necessary are neatness and firmness. We have before mentioned that the gut on which the flies are dressed should be the very finest, and it is equally necessary that the threads used to connect them be of the same description. The following illustration will assist us in explaining to the reader the proper mode of making up a fly-cast.

The thread of gut on which the tail-fly is dressed is here indicated by the letter *a ;* those on which the bobs or droppers are dressed by *b* and *c*. Commence operations by joining the ends of the threads of gut *a* and *b* together ; you have now a fly at both ends. Next take a thread of gut and join it to *b a*

few inches above the hook, then join the end of *c* to this, and so on till you have got the required number. The gut on which the droppers are dressed thus forms a continuation of the main line, and for this reason they should be dressed on the very longest threads.

.The droppers should hang down from the main line from two and a half to three inches. If the distance is increased they are apt to become ravelled with the main line, and occasion the angler considerable loss of time. The distance between the flies should be from twenty inches to two feet. If it is greater in rough water, the angler may pass over a trout without its seeing any of them, and there is nothing in the sight of two flies at a time calculated to alarm a trout.

Some works, when giving instructions for making a fly-cast, recommend that the first dropper should depend from the main line about three inches, the second, five, and so on, always increasing the distance when a fly is added. Their object, if we understand it aright, being, that in fishing, the flies are to be drawn along the water, so that the main line does not touch it at all, but merely the flies. This discloses a very erroneous method of fly-fishing. No angler with any pretensions to skill ever allows his flies, or even his line, for yards above them, to create a disturbance in the water, nothing being more calculated to alarm a trout than seeing flies or line rippling the surface, which the flies must do if drawn along the water sufficiently fast to keep the main line out of it. A great many different methods of making up fly-casts are practised by anglers. Some append them by loops, but loops make such a show in the water that we never have one in any part of our line, and to have the droppers depended by them we consider perfectly suicidal. Others join the main line together by the single slip-knot, which is drawn asunder, and the end of the thread of gut on which the fly is dressed having had a knot put on it to prevent it from slipping, is inserted, when the knot is drawn together again. In point of neatness this is less objectionable, but is apt to slip, as all single knots are. The neatest and most secure method is the one first described, and all anglers should adopt it.

The number of flies that should be used at a time is a matter upon which great diversity of opinion exists; some anglers never use more than three, while others occasionally use a dozen. If the river is so large that the angler cannot reach the opposite bank, he may use as many as he can throw properly; but if the river can be commanded from bank to bank, the propriety, under any circumstances, of using more than three or four is exceedingly doubtful. In such cases the opposite bank is the place where most trout are to be had, and if a number of flies is used, and they are all kept in the water, justice cannot be done to the tail-fly, which alone reaches the opposite bank, and has therefore the best chance.

The fly-cast should be joined to the casting-line by four or five lengths of picked gut, and the whole line should increase in thickness gradually from the flies to the rod ; it is a great assistance to casting.

The only point connected with this subject which remains to be considered is the rod, and it is a very important one. The rod may be used either double or single handed. If the river is large, and the angler is not wading, a double-handed rod might be advisable ; if he is wading, even in a large river, a single-handed one will be sufficient ; and in all rivers which can be commanded from bank to bank, either by wading or otherwise, it should always be used. For fly-fishing, where light throwing and quick striking are indispensable, a double-handed rod is an unmanageable weapon. With it the angler can neither cast with so much certainty, nor strike so instantaneously when he gets a rise, as with a light single-handed rod. It is also exceedingly difficult to regulate with it the amount of force necessary to fix the hook ; the force necessary to move the rod being exceedingly apt to tear small hooks away from their hold. Besides which, it takes a much longer time to cast, and where repeated casting is necessary, this becomes a serious objection.

A light stiff single-handed rod about ten feet long will be amply sufficient for most waters. Those accustomed to use rods from twelve to thirteen feet may think this much too short, but a stiff rod of this length will throw a line further than one of

thirteen feet, made as supple as they usually are.
And even in rods of the same stiffness, a couple of
feet extra length will not enable the angler to throw
much further from him. For supposing he is using
a line twice the length of his rod, he will have four
feet extra length of line and two of rod, in all six
feet. But then the rod in casting is never held
straight out, but at an angle of about forty-five
degrees ; the line also makes an angle with the water,
so that five feet is the utmost additional command
of water gained, and this is much more than counterbalanced by the facility of casting with the small rod,
and by its lightness ; two feet extra length in a rod
entailing at least a half more weight.

It is quite common among anglers to suppose
that a twelve-foot rod will command twice as much
water as one of six feet, but this is an error ; and
in order to explain this, it is necessary to consider
in what the casting power of a rod consists. The
first power in the casting of a line is the force with
which it is urged forward ; thus, if the angler uses
a great amount of force, his line will go further than
if he uses a less amount. The forward motion is
communicated to the line by the point of the rod, so
that upon the rapidity with which the point of the
rod moves through the air depends the motive
power applied to the line. We think the point of
a six-foot rod may be sent through the air as fast as
that of a twelve-foot one ; and, therefore, if the angler
was standing on an elevation of six feet, he could

throw almost as long a line with the small rod as he could with the large one standing on a level with the water. But standing on the same level he could not do this, because with the short rod the line would come into contact with the water long before it had reached its full length; so that upon the altitude of the point of the rod, or the time the line gets to go forward without touching the water, depends the length of line that can be thrown.

Now, supposing the angler holds both rods in his hand, at a distance of five feet from the ground, the altitude of the point of the six-foot rod will be eleven feet, and of the twelve-foot rod seventeen feet. But as substances fall faster every succeeding moment, instead of the times which the lines take to fall from the respective rods being in the proportion of eleven to seventeen, they will be nearly in the proportion of seven to nine; and since the length of line that can be thrown depends entirely upon the length of time it gets to go forward, seven to nine will also be nearly the proportion of the lengths of line that can be thrown. Now, if twenty-one feet is the utmost length of line that the small rod will throw, the large one will throw twenty-seven, or six feet more. Besides this, there are six feet additional length of rod. But as both rod and line are at an angle with the water, the whole gain will only be about nine feet additional command of water. Taking everything into account, the water commanded by the

H

two rods will be very nearly in the proportion of twenty-five to thirty-five.

We are thus particular, in order to show anglers that the additional power of casting is proportionally less with every foot added, and that a ten-foot rod is really a very serviceable weapon. Even with a rod of nine feet we very rarely have occasion to exert its casting powers to their full extent. Fly-fishing, if properly and quickly done, is hard work; and the angler must on no account use a rod in the least degree heavier or longer than he can thoroughly manage with one hand.

The great essential, however, for the fly-rod is stiffness. We have already, when treating of rods, mentioned the advantages a stiff rod possesses over a supple one; and we may perhaps startle some of our readers, who are accustomed to consider a pliant rod indispensable for fly-fishing, by saying that a much stiffer rod is necessary for this branch of the art than any other. For reasons which will be afterwards shown, the flies should first fall on the water, and as little of the line with them as possible. To accomplish this, considerable force must be employed in casting, and the rod must be stopped pretty suddenly. If this is attempted with a supple rod, it would bend till it almost touched the water, and then recoil, throwing the line only a short distance. A supple rod may answer tolerably for fishing down with the wind, but for fishing up, or fishing any way either against or sideways to the wind, it is perfectly useless.

CHAPTER VI.

AVING in the preceding chapters expressed our opinion, that fly-fishing should be practised up stream, and having mentioned the flies and tackle most suitable for the purpose, we now request the reader's particular attention to the remainder of the subject, as being the most important part of it.

The first point which falls under consideration is the casting of the line. After having put up your rod, drawn off a sufficient quantity of line from your reel, and fastened on your flies ; before commencing, soak the line and flies in the water for a few minutes, as it is no use fishing when the gut is dry, and lying in rebellious curls upon the surface ; and when, should a trout take any of the flies, there is a great risk of its carrying them all away—dry gut being very brittle and apt to break at the knots. When the line is thoroughly soaked, take the rod in your right hand, raise it with sufficient force to make the line go to its full length behind, and then pausing for a moment till it has done so, with a circular motion of the wrist and arm urge the rod forward, rapidly at first, but gradually lessening the speed, so that when it stops, no recoil of the point will take place. The whole motion of the rod in casting should be in the shape of a horse shoe; and care must be taken not to urge the flies forward, till they have gone the full length behind, or you will be apt to crack them off. Many a beginner who cracks off his flies pleases himself with the idea that some trout of large dimensions has carried them away.

The line must be so thrown that the flies will fall first upon the water, and as little of the line with them as possible. If you were to fish up a strong stream, and allow the middle of your line to light first, before you could get it straight and prepared for a rise, your flies would be almost at your feet, and should a trout take one of them on their alighting—the most deadly moment in the whole cast—the chances of hooking it would be exceedingly small. It is very different if the flies light first; the line is then nearly straight from the point of the rod to the flies, and the least motion of the hand is felt almost instantaneously. Again, in fishing nooks, eddies, and comparatively still water, at the opposite sides of strong streams, if any of your line lights in the current it is dragged down, and the flies no sooner touch the water, than they are drawn rapidly away in a most unnatural manner, and without giving the trout time to seize them should they feel inclined.

In order to make the flies light first, considerable force must be employed in casting; and the rod must be kept well up; it should never be allowed to make a lower angle with the water than from forty to forty-five degrees. It is upon this point that beginners fail. Their unavailing efforts to get the line well out are entirely owing to their allowing the point of their rod to go too far down, and to their stopping it too quickly, which makes the point recoil, and stops the line in its forward motion. When the flies are just about alighting on the water, you should slightly raise the point of your rod; this checks their downward motion, and they fall much more softly.

The first advice given to beginners in all treatises upon fly-fishing, is to acquire the art of throwing a long and light line. This practice of throwing a long line is the natural consequence of fishing down stream, and for this method of fishing it is absolutely necessary—the advantage being, that the angler is further away from the trout, and therefore less likely to be seen. As we have already shown, this can only be accomplished in a very limited and imperfect manner by throwing a long line, whereas fishing up secures the object perfectly.

In contradistinction to the maxim of throwing a long line, we advise the angler never to use a long line when a short one will, by any possibility,

answer the purpose. The disadvantages of a long
line are, that too much of it touches the water, and
that it is impossible to throw it as it should be done,
making the flies light first. It is also very difficult
to throw it to any desired spot with certainty—to
cast it neatly behind a stone or under a bank ; besides which, more time is necessary to throw it,
thus wasting that valuable commodity. The greatest
objection to it, however, is its disadvantages in
striking a trout ; a long line lies curved in the
water, and when the angler strikes, it is some time
before the flies move ; the line in fact requires to be
straightened first. When they do move, it is slowly
and without force, and there is little chance of hooking the trout. It is very different with a short line ;
in this case the line is almost straight from the point
of the rod to the flies, and the least motion of the
hand moves the latter immediately. We advise the
angler who is using a long line, and raising but not
hooking a number of trout, to shorten his line, and
he will at once be struck with the difference. We
have invariably found that the nearer we are to our
flies the better we can use them, and the greater is
our chance of hooking a trout when it rises.

The advantages of the second part of the maxim
to throw a light line it is impossible to over-estimate.
The moment the flies light—being the only one in
which trout take the artificial fly for a live one—is
the most deadly in the whole cast, and consequently
it is of immense importance to make the flies light in

a soft and natural manner. To accomplish this, and to throw with certainty to any spot wished, requires great practice, and even the most practised angler can never make his flies fall so softly as an insect with outspread gauzy wings.

Thin gut, the necessity of which we have advocated so strongly, is exceedingly difficult to cast, as it has little weight to carry it forward, and therefore beginners should use moderately strong gut at first, and as they improve in casting reduce its size.

A difference of opinion exists as to whether a trout should be struck on rising; but in common with the great majority of anglers, we advocate immediate striking. When a trout takes a fly it shuts its mouth, and if the angler strikes then, he is almost sure to bring the hook into contact with its closed jaws. We have frequently watched the motions of trout on taking a fly, and when left to do with it what they choose, they very quickly expelled it from their mouths with considerable force; and we think that if the angler strikes even when the trout's mouth is open, he will have much better chance than by leaving it to hook itself. A trout on seizing an artificial fly is almost instantaneously aware that it is counterfeit, and never attempts to swallow it, very frequently letting it go before the angler has time to strike; so that it is of the utmost importance to strike immediately, and this is the reason why a quick eye and a ready hand are considered the most necessary qualifications for a fly-

fisher. A trout first takes a fly, and then makes
the motion which anglers term a rise, and which
consists of their turning to go down ; the angler
therefore does not see the least break on the surface
until the trout has either seized or missed the fly,
so that he has already lost so much time, and should
strike immediately.

Although it is impossible to strike too soon, it is
quite possible to strike too hard. Some anglers
strike with such force as to pull the trout out of the
water, and throw it a considerable distance behind
them. Now this is much too hard, and very apt
with a small hook to tear it away from its hold,
should it have any. Striking should be done by a
slight but quick motion of the wrist, not by any
motion of the arm. The angler should also take
care to strike in the same direction as his rod is
moving in at the time, for if he raises his rod, or
otherwise alters its direction, the effect will not be
nearly so immediate, and a moment is of the utmost
importance in this matter.

One advantage of striking is, that should the
trout miss the fly it rises at, the angler has still a
chance of coming across it with some of the remaining ones. In a day's fishing we have frequently
killed half-a-dozen trout hooked by the sides and
other parts. And a trout hooked in this way always
runs twice as hard as one hooked in the mouth.
When hooked in the mouth, the strain that is kept
on it prevents it from moving its gills, and suffo-

cation ensues. This takes place sooner when the trout is drawn down a strong stream; so that the popular notion of pulling a trout down the water to drown it is correct, though the word is rather misapplied. If the trout is hooked by the outside of the body, the respiratory organs are left free, enabling it to run a long time; and when it does come to the side, the angler is disappointed at the small size of a fish which has been making such a desperate struggle.

In fishing up, the rise of a trout is by no means so distinct as in fishing down. They frequently seize the fly without breaking the surface, and the first intimation the angler gets of their presence is a slight pull at the line. The utmost attention is therefore necessary to strike the moment the least motion is either seen or felt. This is in some measure owing to the flies being in general a little under water, but principally to the fact that trout take a fly coming down stream in a quieter and more deadly manner than a fly going up. Seeing it going across and up stream, they seem afraid it may escape, make a rush at it, and in their hurry to seize, very frequently miss it altogether. It is very different in angling up stream : the trout see the fly coming towards them, rise to meet it, and seize it without any dash, but in a firm deadly manner.

When you hook a trout, if it is a small one and you are not wading, pull it on shore at once; if you are wading, it is better to act upon the maxim that "a bird in the hand is worth two in the bush," and come on shore before taking it off the hook, as it is very dangerous doing so when in the water. When you hook a large trout, which you cannot pull on shore at once, but require to exhaust previously, pull it down stream, as, in addition to choking it sooner, you have the force of the current in your favour. In playing a trout, do so as much as possible by keeping up with it by walking, and never let out line if you can avoid it. It is obvious that with a long line you cannot have the same command over it as with a short one ; and take care never to allow your line to get slack, as if you do, and the hook is not fixed, but merely resting on some bone, a thing which frequently occurs, the trout will throw it out of its mouth. To leave this point, in taking the trout out of the water do so with your hands, if you have not a landing-net ; and never attempt lifting it by the line, or you are almost certain to pay dearly for your experience.

When you are approaching a pool which you intend to fish, if the water is clear do so carefully ; you must recollect that the trout see you much more readily if you are on a high bank than if you are on a level with the water. For this reason keep as low down as possible, and always, if the nature of the ground will admit of it, stand a few yards from the edge of the water. If there is a ripple on the water you may meet with good sport

in the still water at the foot of the pools, but if
there is no wind, it is useless commencing till you
come to where the water is agitated.   If you do
not intend fishing the lower part, do not walk up
the side of it, as by so doing you will alarm the
trout in that portion, and they may run up to the
head of the pool for shelter, and frighten the others;
but always come to the edge of the pool at the
place where you intend to begin fishing.   If the
water is very low and the sun bright, it may be
advisable to kneel in fishing a pool, in order to
keep out of sight, and you must avoid allowing your
shadow to fall upon the water above where you are
standing.

First, as you approach, fish the side on which
you are standing with a cast or two, and then commence to fish the opposite side, where you are to
expect the most sport.   For this reason you should
always keep on the shallow side of the water, as
the best trout generally lie under the bank at the
deep side.   After having taken a cast or two on the
near side, throw your flies partly up stream and
partly across, but more across than up, from where
you are standing.   You should throw them to
within an inch of the opposite bank; if they alight
on it so much the better; draw them gently off,
and they will fall like a snow-flake, and if there is
a trout within sight they are almost sure to captivate
it.   In this way your flies will fall more like a
natural insect than by any other method.

After your flies alight, allow them to float
gently down stream for a yard or two, taking care
that neither they nor the line ripple the surface
There is no occasion for keeping them on the surface.
they will be quite as attractive a few inches under
water. As the flies come down stream, raise the
point of your rod, so as to keep your line straight,
and as little of it in the water as possible ; and
when they have traversed a few yards of water,
throw again about a yard or two higher up than
where your flies alighted the previous cast, and so
on. Unless the spot looks exceedingly promising
you need not cast twice in one place if you do not
get a rise, but if there is any quick turn in the
water where there is likely to be a good trout, we
frequently cast over it six or seven times in succession, just allowing the flies to alight when we cast
again. Where the current is strong, the trout may
not see the fly at first, and so we cast repeatedly to
make sure ; and we have frequently, after casting
unsuccessfully half-a-dozen times over the same
place, caught a good trout at last. Move up the
pool as quickly as you can, first taking a cast or
two straight up on the side you are on, and then
fishing the opposite side, and so on, until you finish
the pool. Although it is about the edges of the
pool you will generally get most trout, the main
current must by no means be neglected ; indeed in
it you will frequently capture the best fish. By
fishing in the way we have described, throwing a

yard or two further up every cast, the flies may be
brought in a wonderfully short space of time over
every foot of water where a trout is likely to be.

Streams should be fished in exactly the same
manner as pools ; fishing the side you are on straight
up, and the opposite side partly across and partly
up. All quiet water between two streams, and
eddies behind stones, should be fished straight up,
and the flies just allowed to remain sufficiently long
to let the trout see them ; and in fishing such places
care must be taken to keep the line out of the
current. It is more difficult fishing streams than
pools, as it requires greater nicety in casting ; and
on account of the roughness of the water it is not so
easy to see a trout rise.

In fishing still water with no breeze upon it
you should wait until the motion of the line falling
has subsided, and then draw the flies slowly towards
you ; as, if they were allowed to remain stationary,
the trout would at once detect their artificial nature.

Casting partly across and partly up stream, for
a variety of reasons, is more deadly than casting
directly up. The advantage of having a number of
flies is entirely lost by casting straight up, as they
all come down in a line, and it is only the trout in
that line that can see them ; whereas if thrown
partly across, they all come down in different lines,
and the trout in all these lines may see them. In
casting across, when the flies light, the stream carries
them out at right angles to the line, and they come

down the stream first, so that the trout sees the flies before the line; whereas, in casting straight up, if a trout is between the angler and the place where his flies light, the line passes over it before it sees the flies, and may alarm it.

The moment the fly alights, being the most deadly of the whole cast, it is obvious that the oftener it is repeated the better, and therefore the angler should cast as frequently as possible, always allowing the flies to remain a few moments in order to let the trout see them; but there is not much danger of casting too often, or even casting often enough, as the angler's arm will quickly rebel against it.

Rivers which can be commanded from bank to bank, either by wading or otherwise, constitute by far the most agreeable fishing; but if the river is so large that you cannot reach the opposite side, you must look for sport on the side you are on. And in this case, though you should neglect no spot where a trout may be lying, fish most carefully the part of the pool where the shallow merges into the deep, and where the current is moderately strong; fishing it in the same manner as you would do the opposite side, and always as you go up taking a cast or two straight up, as close to the edge as possible.

On all occasions cast your flies about a yard above where you think the trout are likely to be found, as if on alighting it attracts their attention, there is much less chance of their discovering its artificial nature at that distance. For the same reason, if you see a trout rise at a natural fly, throw above it, and in general it will meet the fly half-way. If a trout rise and you miss it, cast again, and continue doing so until it ceases to rise ; a small trout will frequently rise four or five times in succession ; but the large well-conditioned fish are more wary, and if they miss once or twice will some-times decline returning, however temptingly you may throw your flies.

A breezy day is generally considered favourable for fly-fishing, and no doubt it is so if the wind is blowing up stream ; but it is equally likely that it may be blowing down—it generally blows either up or down, very seldom across—in which case the angler would be very much better without it. Because the wind is blowing down, the angler should on no account fish in the same direction, but must endeavour to cast against it as well as he can. He may, however, stand a little further back from the water, and fish more nearly opposite to where he is standing than would otherwise be advis-able. To cast against the wind, it is necessary to use great force, and immerse a considerable portion of the line in the water. If the wind is very strong, it is a great nuisance, no matter which way it is blowing, as it is sometimes almost impossible to keep the line in the water. In such circumstances it is impossible to fish the streams properly, and the angler should limit his operations to the pools, and should use thicker gut and a heavier casting-line, which will be found a great assistance to casting. It is in such a case that the thorough worthlessness of a supple rod becomes apparent.

As the trout seldom take fly readily for more than four or five hours in the forenoon, you must make the most of the time, fish quickly, walk over the intervening ground smartly, take the trout off the hook, and basket them as speedily as possible, and in every way economise time. If you ever see a professional angler at work when the trout are taking, watch him, and you will be able to form some idea of how expeditiously fishing may be done. As long as you are fishing, do it as if you expected a rise every cast; we have lost many a good trout in an inadvertent moment. If you are tired, or the trout are not taking, sit down and console yourself in some way or other. A late writer upon the subject suggests, that for this purpose the angler should carry a New Testament in his pocket, to which there can be no possible objection, but we rather think most anglers prefer spiritual consolation of a very different sort, coupled with sandwiches; there is a time for all things, and at noon we must admit having a preference for the latter method. It has moreover this advantage, that you will be the more able to fish properly when the trout begin to take again.

We have as yet said nothing about the adapta-

tion of flies in point of size to the season of the year
and the state of the water, because this subject is so
intimately connected with the habits of the trout
during the different fly-fishing months, that it is
impossible to separate them, and we shall therefore
discuss them together; but before commencing, we
may remark, that a knowledge of the habits of the
trout is the most necessary of all information to the
angler.   He may have the best tackle and the best
flies, and be skilled in the art of throwing them
lightly ; but unless he knows where feeding trout
are to be found, he will never achieve great success.

The two great causes which should regulate
the angler in selecting the size of fly to be used are
the colour and size of the water, and the wariness of
the trout ; the fly, in fact, *must be large enough to
ensure its being seen, but not so large as to enable the
trout to detect its artificial nature.*   When a river
is large and dark-coloured, flies may be used a size
or two larger than when it is clear ; as in such circumstances it requires larger flies in order to be
seen, and the thickness of the water prevents trout
from detecting their artificial nature, as they would
if the water was clear.   In a dark windy day, a size
or two larger may be used than in a calm sunny one,
as the roughness of the water and the darkness of
the sky prevent trout from seeing the flies so distinctly ; therefore, the clearer the water and brighter
the day, the smaller should the fly be, and the
thicker the water and darker the day, the larger

I

should it be; always increasing or diminishing the
fly as circumstances prevent its being easily seen, or
the reverse.

Where trout are not much fished for larger flies
may be used than where the reverse is the case, as
the trout, under these circumstances, get suspicious,
and look twice at a fly before they take it. The
reason why shy trout will take a small fly more
readily than a large one is, that since they cannot
see it so distinctly, its artificial nature is not so
easily detected. In streams where the trout are
very shy we generally find that the very smallest
fly raises most fish.

When commencing a day's fly-fishing at any
season, the angler should begin with three or four
different varieties—say a black spider for the tail-
fly, a woodcock wing with yellow silk and red hackle
for the first dropper, a hare-lug body and corn-
bunting wing for the second dropper, and a dun-
coloured spider for the fourth fly. It will be found
advisable, if the trout evince a decided preference
for any of them, to put on two or three of that sort,
leaving on one of a different colour in case of any
change in the humour of the fish, which, however,
rarely happens. We have invariably found ourselves gainers by adopting this method, and that the
droppers which had before been doing little killed
their due proportion when changed to the taking fly.

In order to ascertain the relative value of the
tail-fly and the droppers, we fished for a succession

of days with three flies of exactly the same size, colour, and shape, and tied upon gut of the same thickness. At the conclusion, the proportion stood, 3, 2, 2, the droppers thus capturing the same number, and the tail-fly a half more than either of them. We also fished for several days with four flies of the same kind, when the proportion was, 12, 7, 6, 8. The tail-fly has the best chance, because in casting to the opposite bank where the most trout are taken with the fly, it alone reaches it. The gut is also only on one side of it, whereas the others have gut on both sides. It will be seen that after the tail-fly, the dropper nearest the line has the next best chance, which we ascribe to its being nearest the bank when casting on the same side of the water on which we were standing. The foregoing trials were made with the view of ascertaining when a fly is not doing its duty and ought to be changed ; they were all conducted in a river which could be commanded from bank to bank. In a large river we should suppose that the proportions would be slightly different, and that the tail-fly would not kill so much in proportion.

The time of year when trout begin to take fly readily entirely depends upon the nature of the river and the season. They never rise freely at the artificial fly until they are accustomed to feed upon the natural insect ; and the first insects which make their appearance in any quantity are the March browns. It is not until these flies have been a week or ten days on the water, or at a time, varying.

according to the season and district from the middle
to the end of April, that fly-fishing really commences. In that short space of time trout improve
wonderfully in condition, and leaving the still water,
where they have had their haunts during winter,
move up into the stronger parts of the pools, about
the sides of which they lie in wait for their prey.

If the weather is mild, which it rarely is at this
season of east winds, the end of April is the best
fly-fishing time of the whole season. The trout take
with a readiness and certainty which they never
exhibit at any subsequent period. Flies are still a
rarity to them, and they are not yet shy from being
over-fed, or from a frequent view or more practical
experience of artificial flies. Other reasons why
more trout can be captured with the fly at this season
than any other are, that there are more trout in the
water—the summer's fishing and netting not having
begun yet,—and that the trout are more concentrated
in particular places.

As regards the imitation of the March brown,
which is held in such high estimation amongst anglers,
if the water is heavy, trout will sometimes take it
readily, not because they see any resemblance between it and the real March brown—at least we
never could—but because it is a good size of fly for
the season ; any of the flies we have mentioned,
dressed of the same size, will be equally killing.
The flies used this month should in general be full
size ; if the waters are coloured, Nos. 9 and 10 will

be found most effective ; but if the waters are small, a size or two less will be advisable.

At this season a warm sunny day is most favourable to the angler. The birth of flies depends in a great measure upon the state of the weather ; and when there are no natural flies on the water trout never rise freely at an artificial one. An east wind or a cold frosty day is a death-blow to the angler's hopes, as in such there are no flies to be seen, and the trout retire to deep water. In this month we have frequently seen, about eleven o'clock in the forenoon, a perfect shower of March browns come on the water, which for half-an-hour or so appeared almost boiling with trout leaping ; and then the flies went off and all was quiet again. Till the flies appeared we met with no sport ; when they were on the water we got a rise almost every cast, and when they went away we hardly got another trout.

This is what is popularly known as "the time of the take," and occurs, more or less, at some time of the day the whole season through. The leaping of the trout in all directions at once informs the angler when it commences, and he should make the most of his time. It sometimes happens several times during the day, but rarely lasts more than an hour at a time, and stops as suddenly as it commences. It is only during the take that a trout can be caught in very deep water, as it is only then they are hovering near the surface on the outlook for flies. Once it is over they retire to the bottom and there lie ; and if the water is very deep they may not be able to see the angler's flies, or if they do, cannot be troubled to rise to seize them ; so that when trout are not taking freely, the angler will always meet with most success in comparatively shallow water.

In April the angler must look for sport in the pools, as the trout are not yet strong enough to lie in the streams, and therefore it is of no use fishing in them. There are some parts of a pool in which trout are, at all seasons, more likely to be found than in others. There are always plenty of them lying in the shallow water at the pool-foot, which, if there is a ripple on it, will be found the best place of all. Passing up to the deeper portions of the pool, the trout are more congregated about the sides, as it is there that the aquatic insects on which they feed are most numerous. They choose convenient feeding stations below some large stone or tuft of grass, where the river runs beneath the bank, or where a projecting bush affords food and shelter to some finny giant who holds his revels below. Such places are always sure to be tenanted, and what is rather singular, the best feeding station in a pool or stream is generally occupied by the largest trout in it, and if it is captured the next largest takes its place ; and we have day after day caught a trout in one spot, each capture being of smaller dimensions than its predecessor.

In cold weather, in the early part of the season,

we have generally found the sunny side of the water the best ; we suppose because there are more insects there.

Passing from April to May, trout improve greatly in condition, and move into stronger water about the heads of pools, scattering themselves, but not plentifully as yet, through the streams. Of all places where the angler is likely to find trout at any season, the meeting of two streams is the best ; there in the quiet water between and on either side of the strong runs, feeding trout are sure to be lying, watching to seize whatever the stream brings in the way of food. Such places should always be fished with great care.

For fishing slow-running streams, the end of April and beginning of May are the best times, and the trout in such are then in excellent condition ; but for rivers in general, the month of May, taking it as a whole, is worth any two months to the flyfisher. Sport may be more relied upon than in the preceding month. The birth and appearance of flies on the water is rendered less dependent on the weather ; a cold day or an east wind does not do the same mischief, and the trout will generally take during the whole day, unless the weather is extremely cold. We have never at this season found it of any use to attempt fly-fishing before seven or eight in the morning ; the forenoon, from eight till about noon, or an hour or two after, we consider the best time ; about two they generally leave off taking, but commence again in the evening, if the weather is mild. In the beginning of the month we have generally met with most success in a warm sunny day ; but to tell the most favourable weather with anything like certainty is impossible, as the trout are very capricious, and will sometimes take readily during a hail-storm, while at other times, in such a case, not a trout will rise. Towards the end of the month we prefer a showery day with west wind, or a thoroughly wet one if the weather is warm.

The best condition of water for capturing trout is when there is just sufficient rain to raise the water slightly, and make it of an amber colour. When a large flood occurs, it scatters the trout too much, and they become gorged with food, and do not take so readily ; so that more trout can generally be caught in a clear water than after a heavy flood. If the water is only coloured or slightly swollen, trout will be found in the same places as when it is clear ; but when the water is large and dark-coloured it is of no use fishing the streams, as they are too rapid, and in the pools the trout are all congregated about the sides. In such circumstances, therefore, the angler should not waste time fishing the centre of the pool, but merely fish the sides ; fishing the side he is on straight up and as close to the edge as possible, and the opposite side partly across and partly up as usual. The greatest number will frequently be got on the thin side, but the largest and best trout are almost invariably caught on the deep side, and very close to the edge.

The flies used in May should be smaller than those used in April; if the waters are clear, No. 11 or 12 will answer very well, but if the rivers are coloured, a size larger may be used; a good-sized fly will frequently catch the best trout in heavy water.

Towards the end of this month the stone-fly, or May-fly of Tweedside, makes its appearance— the green drake to which the name of May-fly is usually applied not appearing for a fortnight later. These flies give the first great blow to artificial fly-fishing; they are so large, and the trout get them in such abundance, that before they have been many days on the water, the trout become quite satiated with surface food. They are now in prime condition—strong and vigorous—affording excellent play when hooked. They also forsake the deeper portions of the pools, moving up into the strong water at the head, and into broken water and streams, where they choose convenient feeding stations, such as eddies behind stones, below banks, and submersed tufts of grass, and, in short, every place where they can remain unseen, and watch for their prey as it comes down stream towards them; and the angler should neglect no place where he thinks there is a trout.

About this time they begin to act the epicure, becoming exceedingly nice in their tastes, and pay-ing little attention to the angler's lure, and they may frequently be seen following, without making any attempt to seize it. When they are in this mood, which generally lasts till the beginning of August, always use spiders, and reduce their size to No. 12 or 13 ; a No. 14 midge may also be used with advantage. This, to a certain extent, meets their views, it being more suspicion of the nature of the fly, thɑn want of inclination to seize it, which makes them so nice. On such occasions also, the angler should pass over the pools, and fish the streams, as in them, owing to the roughness of the water, the trout cannot so easily detect the artificial nature of the flies.

From the middle of June to the beginning of August is the worst part of the whole season for fly-fishing. In large rivers, such as Tweed, and all slow-running streams, fly-fishing—at least during the day—is not worth practising. At sunset, however, trout will rise freely, and continue to do so all night, if the weather is favourable. A dry, warm night, with little dew falling, will generally be found most favourable ; if there is much dew falling, or a thick mist rising from the water—the surrounding country being free from it—trout will not take freely. At night they leave the streams and pool-heads, to cruise about among the pool-foots and shallows, and it is in these places that the angler should fish for them. Two flies will gene- rally be found sufficient for night-fishing, and they should be a good deal larger than those used during the day. The largest trout caught during the summer months are usually taken at night, as it is only then that they leave the bottom of the deep pools in search of food.

At this season the fly-fisher, in search of sport during the day, should have recourse to the smaller waters and more backward districts of the country, where the trout are not yet—indeed in some places they never are—satiated with surface food. Fly-fishing at this season is more difficult than at any other, for unless in a very favourable day, the trout will not rise in the pools; the angler, therefore, must have recourse to the streams and rough broken water, and to fish these successfully with the fly is very nice practice indeed. The flies alone should touch the water, and they should never be thrown into the main current, but into nooks and eddies, and all those places where the worm-fisher would look for sport, and which will be indicated in a subsequent chapter. The trout that will take a worm will generally rise at a spider, if thrown lightly over it; but in fly-fishing the angler cannot capture one-fourth of the trout that rise, whereas in worm-fishing he can make sure of one out of two offers, which accounts for the comparatively few trout in the fly-fisher's basket at this season.

In clear sunny days, trout may frequently be seen basking in shallow water, which, at first sight, seems scarcely sufficient to cover them. On such occasions they will rise greedily at a spider, if the angler keeps well out of sight, and throws lightly over them ; he must also take care that the shadow of his rod does not fall upon the water in their neigh-bourhood.   The capture of one will, however, scare away the others, and they will not return for some time.

Trout will rarely, even in the heat of summer, take fly readily early in the morning ; they generally commence about six, and continue taking for four or five hours, when they stop for some time ; com-mencing again in the evening, if the weather is favourable.   At all seasons, the forenoon is the best time, unless, perhaps, in June and July, when they will take most freely about sunset.

The atmosphere at this season is frequently in a calm thundery state, with heavy white clouds floating about, which is not favourable to the angler. From the end of May to the end of August, a drizz-ling or thoroughly wet day is the best ; next to which is a showery one, and then a bright day with a breeze of wind ; a dark day without wind is the worst of all.   East wind, which is looked upon with so much horror at the commencement of the season, is not at all objectionable now ; being rather favourable than otherwise, as it is generally accompanied with a cool atmosphere.

In July we have always met with even less sport when the water was coloured than when it was clear, which we can only account for by supposing, that as it is the worm season, the trout are on the outlook for this description of food, and pay no attention to the flies; at least in such circumstances we never see many rises at the natural insect.

In the summer months it is considered a great improvement to hook a maggot to the end of the fly, but this is not fly-fishing, and changes the character of the lure from the most clean and pleasant to the most disagreeable of all the methods of capturing trout. It has, moreover, at all times a substitute in a fine red worm, which is much more agreeable to handle, and will kill two for one which the fly with the maggot will.

August is a better month for the fly than July, and during the whole of it, but especially at the latter end, trout rise freely. Night-fishing may now be said to be at an end; the nights in general are cold and frosty, and the trout will not rise freely; so that there is little inducement to leave a comfortable bed to shiver at the water-side. By the beginning of September there is a visible change for the worse in the condition of the trout—they are full of spawn, and are fast losing strength, firmness, and flavour. They now commence to leave the streams, and return to the pools and more quiet water; it is worthy of remark, that those which remain in the streams are generally in good condition; if they were not, they would not have strength to keep their place in strong water. The flies used this month, as well as in the end of August, should be a size or two larger than those used during summer—approaching in size to a spring fly. After a flood capital sport may be had; the trout will rise almost as freely as in the month of May, and though in general out of condition, the angler will still meet with some that will test freely both his skill and tackle. They will continue taking through October, but excepting the small ones, are in such poor condition, as to be totally unfit for use.

The sizes of flies we have indicated are those suitable for southern streams. In highland rivers, where the trout are not so numerous or wary, flies considerably larger than those we have mentioned will frequently secure the best trout.

Fly-fishing in streams inhabited by cunning, cautious trout, when the water is low and clear, is undoubtedly the kind of fishing which requires most science. And for our own part we would rather capture ten pounds weight of trout in some much-fished southern stream open to the public, than twice that quantity in some preserved water, or remote highland stream, where the trout seldom see an artificial fly, and are ready to seize anything that presents itself in the shape of food. Fishing in preserved water loses a great part of its pleasure. We like to be free to seek trout where we like, and take them where we can; and as there is more merit, there is more pleasure, in filling a basket where all

anglers, high and low, rich and poor, are free to do
the same, than in a river fished only by a favoured
few.   All beginners in the art, if they wish to excel,
should commence in streams where the trout are
remarkably shy, and they will the sooner become
skilful. If they commence in highland streams, where
the trout are half-starved, and where it requires
little exercise of skill to capture them, they will
get into a careless style of fishing, which they may
find it difficult to alter.   We have known anglers
from the north, who considered themselves, and
were considered, good fishers, and who in their own
streams could kill seven or eight dozen trout in a
day, unable to secure half-a-dozen small fish in our
southern streams.   The angler who can kill trout in
streams such as Tweed, Gala, or Almond, which are
fished by dozens every day, may rest assured that
he is quite able to kill them wherever they are to
be found.

CHAPTER VII.

ISHING with the worm is not usually held in such high estimation as it deserves ; a circumstance entirely owing to its being but very imperfectly understood. Fly-fishers are apt to sneer at worm-fishing as a thing so simple that any one may succeed in it—their notions of it being that it is practised either when the waters are swollen after rain, or with a float and sinkers in some deep pool ; and it is not surprising that with such ideas of it, they should hold it in contempt. Worm-fishing is only worthy of the name of sport, when practised in streams inhabited by wary trout when they are low and clear. Under such circumstances it becomes a branch of the art, which, to be pursued with success, requires the most intimate acquaintance with the habits of the trout, and the nicest powers of casting ; and which in point of difficulty is only inferior to fly-fishing. Those anglers who despise worm-fishing as a thing so simple as to be quite unworthy of their atten-

tion, would quickly discover their mistake if brought
to a small clear water on a warm sunny day in June
or July.

As a lure for trout, worm unquestionably ranks
next to artificial fly. It also comes in at a very
suitable time—being the very season in which the
fly-fisher meets with least encouragement. One
advantage it possesses over fly is the superior size
of the trout caught; in general they will average
a half more in weight. If any angler is limited
to one week's fishing in the year, he should choose
bright weather and clear water in the beginning
of July; if skilled in the use of the worm, he may
depend upon killing more trout then than any
other week in the year.

The first subject which naturally suggests itself
is the tackle necessary for this mode of fishing.
The rod should be at least four feet longer than
that used for fly.

A double-handed rod should be used on all
occasions, and in all waters, whether small or large.
A single-handed rod is most suitable for fly-fishing,
where quick striking is necessary, and where a line
several times the length of the rod can be thrown
with ease; but in worm-fishing, quick striking is
not necessary, and throwing a long line is highly
reprehensible, as the force required to cast it mutilates
the worm sadly. For this reason also, the rod for
worm-fishing should be rather more pliant, as it
requires more force and a more sudden impulse to

cast a certain length of line with a stiff rod than
with a moderately supple one. As you cannot cast
a long line, keeping out of the trout's sight must be
managed by length of rod, not by length of line ;
and a single-handed rod can never accomplish this
properly. The rod should not be shorter than from
fourteen to sixteen feet. This, with a line from
once to once and a half as long as the rod, is sufficient
to keep the angler out of sight in the clearest water.
The rods made in the fishing-tackle shops for bait-
fishing are generally very well adapted for the purpose, and are not, like the fly-rods, made too supple.

The reel, line, and casting-line should be the
same as those used for fly-fishing ; and the hook
should be joined to the latter by seven or eight
lengths of picked gut. The gut used for this
purpose, as well as for dressing the hooks on,
should be the very finest that can be had. An
opinion is quite current among anglers, that fine
gut is by no means necessary for bait-fishing ; and
when assorting a hank, they lay aside the fine
threads for fly, and the remainder for bait. This is
a great mistake—fine gut being equally necessary
for both methods. We once, on passing over a
bridge, when returning from a day's fishing, observed
a trout of about a pound weight basking in the sun,
in water not half-a-foot deep. Wishing to ascertain
if he was inclined to take a worm, we threw one
in a little above him. This he devoured eagerly, as
also another. We then baited our hook and threw

it in above him ; but on its approaching he made off
very quickly, being evidently alarmed by the gut.

In dressing bait-hooks, take a well-waxed red
silk thread, and commence by giving it a turn or
two round the end of the shank of the hook, to prevent the latter from cutting the gut ; then laying the
gut to the hook, whip both firmly together rather
more than half-way up the shank, where finish with
a succession of hitch-knots or the whip-fastening.

With regard to the size of hook, we think a
small size, not larger than No. 3 or 4, is best, being
much more easily swallowed, and less likely to be
discovered by the trout. When baiting, take the
hook, and entering it close to the head end of the
worm, run the worm up on it and on the gut, till it
is all impaled but about three-quarters of an inch of
the tail, which should be left to play about. The
object of this is, that the trout, which always makes
its first attack upon the part which appears most lively,
may seize the end where the hook is. It is the
practice of some anglers to leave a large part of the
head to move about, under the supposition that the
worm will live longer. This is very objectionable,
as in such circumstances the trout may make its first
attack on the head, and may be alarmed by getting
the gut in its mouth ; or the angler may strike
before it takes hold of the hook at all, and consequently lose the trout.

With every precaution, however, the angler will
sometimes miss three or four trout in succession,

because they have not the hook in their mouth, but merely bite some part of the worm. In such circumstances three or four small hooks about No. 9 or 10 of Bartlett's, or what are perhaps even better, three of Hutchinson and Son's sneck-bent hooks, No. 3 or 4, tied to one thread of gut, will be found much more effective than a single hook.

The accompanying illustration shows the tackle

and the method of baiting it, which requires no explanation.

The advantages of this tackle are—that a trout can hardly take hold of the worm at all without having one of the hooks in its mouth ; that the worm lives much longer, and being free to wriggle itself into any shape, is more natural-looking and consequently enticing; and lastly, that it is much more easily baited, particularly if the worms are fresh. Its disadvantages are—that it is more difficult to extricate from the trout's mouth ; that it requires to be baited afresh every bite ; and that the exposure of so many hooks is calculated to scare away some trout that would otherwise take the bait. But, upon the whole, the advantages preponderate considerably over the disadvantages, particularly when trout are biting shy.

From using this tackle occasionally and finding it answer, we were led to think that by using it continually more trout might be captured than with the common bait-hook. We resolved to devote three successive days in order to test this, and to fish one half-hour with the common hook, and the next with three or four small ones ; varying the number and size to suit the worms. The first trial was in Gala, between Bowland and Stow, where the trout are of good size and remarkably wary ; so that the exposure of the hooks would tell with full force. On this occasion we captured 20½ lbs. of trout, of which 9½ lbs. were taken with the common hook and 11 lbs. with the tackle. The next trial was in Leader, between Earlston and Lauder, when we captured with the common hook 14½ lbs., and with the tackle 17½ lbs. The third day was also in Leader, when the result was with the common hook 12½ lbs., and with the tackle 13½ lbs.—making a total during the three days of 36½ lbs. with the common hook, and 42 lbs. with the tackle ; leaving a difference in favour of the latter of 5½ lbs., or about fifteen per cent. Had we been fishing all these days with the single hook we should only have had 19 lbs., 29 lbs., and 25 lbs. respectively ; whereas, had we fished continually with the tackle, we should have had 22 lbs., 35 lbs., and 27 lbs.— no small difference. All these trials were made in the middle of July, when the waters were very small and clear, and consequently when every objection that can be urged against the four hooks was likely to tell with full force; added to which, the stones, as is frequently the case after long-continued dry weather, were covered with green slimy vegetable matter, which stuck to the small hooks whenever they came in contact with it, and occasioned considerable loss of time.

A brother of the writer made the same trial with the same result. He also observed that with the tackle he got fewer trout, but larger ones, which seems surprising, but may be accounted for by supposing that though some trout had been alarmed by the exposure of the hooks, the lively and natural appearance of the worm had been more attractive to large trout. Whether or not every angler will meet with the same result, *entirely depends upon his capabilities for baiting and managing the respective tackles;* but probably all really good anglers will catch more weight of trout with the three or four small hooks than with the one large one; and since we first introduced it to the attention of anglers four years ago, it has come into very general use.

Whatever kind of hooks the angler is using, he should pay great attention to the state of his worm, and if it has become maimed or water-logged, change it, as a lively worm is more enticing than a dead one.

Split shot to regulate the rate of the worm down stream are usually considered indispensable by the angler; but, except on rare occasions, impeding the motion of the worm is objectionable, and for the following reasons :—A worm thrown into a stream would be carried down by the current and turned round in every eddy ; and as this is the way in which trout are accustomed to see worms coming down stream, every deviation from it is calculated to excite their suspicion. When there are two or three split shot on the line, the worm travels at a slower rate than the stream, and yields but little to any eddy. The shot control and retard its movements, so that, looking upon the shot as almost stationary, the line between them and the worm, and of course the worm itself at the end of it, are dangling about in the stream ; in fact, to a certain extent, resisting the current, instead of being carried down by it. Again, if the worm is thrown into an eddy, the shot go to the bottom and lie there ; but the worm, being much lighter, rises with the current as far as the length of line between it and the shot, and there remains almost stationary. Now, in both these cases, the shot give an unnatural motion to the worm.

The alleged advantages of shotting are, that the worm travels more slowly, affording the trout plenty of time to seize it, and that it always reaches the bottom. Now, as to the first assertion, the best rate for the worm to travel at is undoubtedly the natural one, and if the trout wish to seize it, they have always plenty of time to do so. To the second reason we attach some importance ; it is natural for the worm to be near the bottom, and with sinkers the angler will certainly catch trout in deeper water than he could without them, but as a rule it is not in deep water that the worm-fisher must look for sport ; and in water not above a couple of feet deep, the worm will reach the bottom very quickly without any assistance ; and even should it not, the trout will rise to seize it, frequently jumping at it as they would at a fly. The only occasions in which the use of sinkers can be defended are, either when the wind is blowing so strong that it would be impossible to keep the line in the water without them, or when it is necessary to fish water so deep that the trout would not see the worm unless they were used.

Besides giving an unnatural motion to the worm, sinkers are highly objectionable in other respects. They are constantly hanking below stones, and occasioning the angler a great deal of annoyance and loss of time. With them also the angler gets over the ground at a much slower rate than when · his worm comes down almost at the same rate as the stream. This opinion about sinkers is held by almost all the best worm-fishers ; and some Tweed-side adepts never use them under any circumstances.

Many different kinds of worms are used by the angler, but the four following are held in highest estimation, and are also to be found in greatest abundance. In Edinburgh they may be had ready for use at a very moderate price ; but in country places the angler will frequently require to dig and prepare his own bait, or he will be but indifferently provided, and therefore it behoves him to know the places where he may find them, and how to prepare them.

THE BLACK-HEADED WORM.—This worm is usually found in good garden soil, or among heaps of decayed rubbish, and may be known by being free from the knot which most worms have. As its name signifies, it has a black head, and when taken from the earth is of a darkish colour throughout, which it loses when scoured, becoming of a clear reddish tinge, and is a very inviting worm to look at. As an angling bait it deserves the first rank, being the most durable of all worms. The only objections to it are—the length of time it takes to scour, and the difficulty of getting any number of a proper size.

THE BRANDLING is only to be found in an old dunghill or similar place, and it may be known by being ringed all round, with a knot a little above the middle : it is also flatter in shape than most worms. We hold this worm in great repute ; it can be scoured in a day or two, and is then a beautiful worm to appearance. It is also in general of the very size the angler would wish. The principal objection to brandlings is their extreme softness ; they are incapable of being toughened, and when used upon a single hook, slip down upon the bend, thus exposing the shank. This objection does not apply to them when used upon the four small hooks, and we very often use them in this way.

When pierced they emit a very offensive smell, but anglers must not be too particular in this respect.

THE MARSH WORM.—When taken from the earth this worm is of a pale-blue colour, with a whitish knot a little above the centre. It is a very small worm, and is more usually found too small than too large. If kept sufficiently long it becomes of a lively pink colour, and may be used with great success, particularly in small waters. It is the most plentiful of all descriptions of worms, and may be found in any garden among heaps of decayed rubbish and below stones.

THE RED-HEADED WORM.—This worm is only to be found plentifully in the very richest soil, about the edges of dunghills and similar places. It is of a dark-red colour on the head and all down the back, and of a pale-blue colour underneath. As a bait for trout it does not deserve much attention. It is so thick in proportion to its length, that if it is sufficiently long to cover the hook, it makes too large a bait, and after it has been a very short time in the water it loses its colour, becoming quite dark, and consequently not so attractive.

With regard to the size of worm for fishing where the trout are well fed and wary when the waters are clear, worms can hardly be used too small if they cover the hook. A worm from two to three inches long, and about the thickness of a hen's quill, is the largest size that should be used. A small bright clean worm is always most enticing to well-fed trout; and it is quite common to meet anglers using worms so large as effectually to prevent their having the least sport. It is a great error to suppose that a large worm insures a large trout; quite the reverse. A large worm will seldom capture anything but some audacious little fellow of a parr, or equally insignificant trout.

Trout do not seem to evince any decided preference for one kind of worm before another, so that the angler may use whichever kind he likes best or can get most easily. The great point is to have them of the right size and well scoured. When newly dug, they are so full of earth as to be unfit for use. Brandlings may be scoured in a day or two; but the other kinds require to be kept at least a week. Immediately on being dug, they should be washed in water, and put into an earthenware jar with plenty of moss. The moss should be well washed, and wrung as hard as possible, and all the small sticks and straws picked carefully out, as they are apt to cut the worms. The jar should be examined every second or third day, and all the dead or sickly worms picked out and the moss changed. The process of toughening worms can only be accomplished by keeping the moss dry, so that the worms may lose some of the moisture of their bodies, and thus become tougher and more durable. This is objectionable, as it impairs the vitality of the worms, giving them, if carried to any extent, a very withered look. When thoroughly

divested of earthy matter, worms can be easily
baited; and they will last quite long enough without
going through the additional process of toughening,
or rather drying. The worm-jar should always be
kept in a cool place.

For containing worms when angling, a flannel
bag, large enough to admit the hand freely, will be
found the most convenient receptacle. It should
have a loop attached to it, by which it may be
fastened to the button of the angler's coat, and a
separate string to tie round the mouth. If the
angler intends fishing long at a time, he will find it
an improvement to divide his worms, keeping one
half in a bag in his basket till required. The
repeated thursting in of the angler's hand, the dangling of the bag, and exposure to the sun, will greatly
injure the worms before the day is out, if the whole
supply is kept in one bag.

The angler should be very particular about the
size and appearance of his worms, and should never
start for a day's trouting without a sufficient supply.
Nothing is more provoking than to run short of bait
at the very time the trout are taking. Under any
circumstances, a gross and a half or two gross is the
smallest number that should be taken for a day's
trouting with worm.

Worm-fishing is better understood than fly-fishing; that is to say, there are more anglers who fish
up stream with the one than with the other. Angling up stream with the worm possesses all the

advantages which have been mentioned in fly-fishing.
and which it is unnecessary to recapitulate. The
objections against fishing down stream apply with
even greater force to worm-fishing than to fly, as in
fly-fishing the angler can keep out of sight, to a
certain extent, by throwing a long line. Not so in
worm-fishing; he must either be opposite or below
his worm, so that every trout in the neighbourhood
of his line can see him distinctly; and if he were
to fish down a small clear water with the worm, he
would hardly catch a trout, while his neighbour fishing up stream might fill his basket. All worm-fishers
of the present day that know anything about the
matter invariably throw their worm up stream.

In trouting with the worm, a proper casting of
the line is of great importance. The two things to
be attended to are, to throw lightly, so as not to
break the worm, and to throw with certainty to any
required spot. To accomplish the first mentioned,
some recommend heaving or pitching the line forward; but this is a very uncertain method, quite
impracticable in a windy day, and hardly practicable
at any time, unless there is plenty of shot on the
line. We do not see that it mutilates the worm
less than the ordinary method; and at best the line
can never be thrown with the same certainty.

In casting a worm, you should allow it to go
out behind, and then urge it forward slowly; all
sudden jerks must be avoided, as they are apt to
tear the worm, and force it down on the bend of

the hook, thus exposing the shank. You must also allow the point of your rod to go nearer the water than in casting a fly, as it is necessary to extend the rod to the full length, in order to get the bait as far out as possible. In doing this, you must not lower the point of your rod till you have given the worm all the forward impetus you intend ; then lower it slowly almost to a level with the water, and the worm will go to the full stretch of both rod and line. Whenever the worm lights, raise your rod gradually, so as to keep as little of your line in the water as possible ; but you must take care not to raise it so quickly as in any way to interfere with the motion of the worm. It is of great importance that there should be very little line in the water, not so much because it is calculated to alarm the trout, as because the action of the stream upon the line will in some cases bring the worm down much faster than it would otherwise come, and in others bring it nearer the surface. If you throw your worm into an eddy or any quiet piece of water at the side of a stream, and any part of the line alights in the current, the worm will be swept out almost instantaneously. When you throw your worm and line into an open stream, the worm, presenting considerable surface to its action, is carried down almost at the same rate as the stream ; but the line, not presenting so much surface to the action of the water, lags behind. If this takes place to any extent, and there is much line further up the stream than the worm, the stream still pressing on the worm, and the line above presenting some resistance to the free progress of the worm down stream, it is brought nearer the surface. To avoid this, the angler should keep his rod a little further down stream than his worm, and should have no part of his line in the water, but four or five feet of the very finest gut, which should now and then be drawn gently down stream, so as to keep as little line above the worm as possible. It is by attending to this that the angler can keep his worm near the bottom ; but it must be done so gently that it will neither pull the worm down stream nor nearer the surface. If this be properly done the angler will catch a half more trout than if he were keeping a large quantity of line immersed in the water. For the length of line, the angler will be guided entirely by circumstances ; but it will rarely be found necessary to use one much longer than the rod.

The first notice you get of a trout's having taken your bait is in general a stoppage of the line. This, however, may arise from the hook or line having come in contact with some fixed object. You should therefore lower the point of your rod down stream till your line is straight, when you will at once know whether or not there is a trout at it. The proper time to strike depends upon whether you are using a common bait-hook or the four-hook tackle. If you are using the latter, strike down stream as soon as you can get your line straight.

If you are using a common bait-hook, it is difficult to know the proper time to strike. You may strike before the trout has the hook in its mouth at all, or you may give it so long that it may discover the hook and expel it from its mouth. In either case you lose the trout. A trout, when taking a worm, frequently seizes the part that is up on the line and quite free from the hooks, and will carry it away to his lair before attempting to swallow it. A pull at the line intimates that a trout has taken the worm ; there is then generally an even pull and running out of the line ; and when this stops, which indicates that the trout has arrived at his starting-place, the angler should strike, and in general he will secure the trout.

You will frequently observe, when you have caught a trout, or even had one on for a moment, that the worm is off the hooks and a considerable distance up the line, sometimes past one or even two knots. This shows that trout must possess some extraordinary power of expelling from their mouths what they find disagreeable, as it is certainly the fish that does it, and not the dangling of the line, or any motion of the stream or rod.

In fishing pools, if the water is very clear and low, approach carefully. In general, it will be found advisable to kneel ; and, as in fly-fishing, you should come to the water-side at the place where you intend commencing, and should also keep on the shallow side of the water. With a line a little longer than your rod, throw your worm gently as far up from you as possible, and allow it to come down nearly opposite to where you are standing, when you should throw again. Casting partly across and partly up is more deadly than casting directly up ; the reason of which is, that in casting directly up, if there is a trout between the angler and the place where the worm lights, all the line passes over it before it sees the bait, and may alarm it. Two casts in one place will in general be sufficient to determine if there is any trout inclined to take ; but if you get a bite, you should of course cast there again.

In fishing streams, cast in the same direction as in fishing pools ; but as the water is rougher, you will not be so easily seen, and kneeling is unnecessary. You should always throw your worm a few yards above where you think a trout is lying, as by the time the bait reaches it, it will be pretty well sunk, and trout take a worm most readily near the bottom. As you will invariably get most trout on the opposite side of the water from where you are standing, always keep on the side where you think there are fewest trout lying. The practice adopted by some anglers of wading up the centre of the stream, and casting on both sides of them, answers very well in large rivers, where there is plenty of water to conceal the angler ; but in small rivers it alarms the trout. Not that the trout, where the angler casts his line, sees him ; but those about the

L

part of the water where he is standing run up and alarm the others. The better plan is to fish the side you are on as you approach, and then, if necessary, wade in to fish the opposite. But on all occasions, make as little disturbance and keep as little line in the water as possible.

With regard to the season when worm-fishing commences, a few trout may be taken with the worm in April and May; but at this season there is no inducement to use it, as trout take fly much more readily; and if the angler must have a bait, he will find a much more deadly one in the May-fly, which forms the subject of the next chapter. There are some anglers who never fish with anything else but worms; a proceeding we can only account for by supposing that they are deficient both in knowledge and taste. When worm-fishing is not in season, the trout captured by it are neither so large nor so well-conditioned as those taken with the fly. Trout never take a worm freely till they are thoroughly satiated with surface-food; and this seldom happens until the May-flies are off the water, or at a time varying from the beginning of June to the beginning of July. It is now that worm-fishing commences in earnest, and really good and exciting sport it is. The trout are in splendid condition, strong and vigorous; so that a half-pound trout at this season will afford as much play as one of twice the size would have done two months earlier. It is the most certain and deadly of all fishing; and by it more trout may be captured in the month of July than by any other means in any other month of the year. And he is not worthy of the name of angler who cannot, in any day of the month, when the water is clear, kill from fifteen to twenty pounds weight of trout in any county in the south of Scotland.

Sport can also be more relied upon in this than in any other kind of angling ; thunder in the air, that dread of the fly-fisher, does little harm here. We never found trout taking better than one day in Gala during a thunder-storm, when we captured 22½ lbs. of trout, and they continued taking as readily as ever, till about one o'clock, when suddenly the water, which before had been clear, came down quite thick and muddy, and put an end to further sport.

The first part of the day is undoubtedly the best, and the angler should arrange so as to have the bulk of his take by twelve o'clock; but if the day is dark, and the sun comes out about four P.M., or a mild shower falls, very good sport may be had up to a late hour in the evening. If the weather is favourable, the angler cannot commence too early ; trout will take readily when there is only sufficient light to bait a hook. A dry morning, with little dew, or a rainy one, if it is warm, will generally be found best ; but if there is much dew falling, or a thick mist rising from the waters, trout will not take till some time after the sun is up. Early in

the morning—that is to say, before six or seven
o'clock—trout will take worm readily in the streamy
portions of the pools, in water where there is not
much chance of success during the day. Numbers
of trout, which have been cruising about the shallows
all night, have not yet returned to the streams, but
are lying in the strong deep water. Morning fishing, however, is very uncertain, and seven o'clock is
quite early enough to start.

If trout have been taking readily in the early
part of the morning, a lull usually takes place for
an hour or so, about six or seven; and if they have
not been taking in the morning, they generally commence about that time. During the day, unless
there is a breeze of wind, little sport is to be had in
the pools ; but if there is a good ripple on them,
very good sport may be had in the shallow water
towards their lower end, as also in stretches of thin
still water, which, at other times, it would be use-·
less fishing. The whole of a pool may be fished
when there is a breeze of wind upon it, but there is
no part like the lower end, where there are always
plenty of trout lying. When there is no wind, the
only part of a pool worth fishing is the strong rush
at the head. The streams, however, are what the
angler should rely upon, and an experienced worm-
fisher can tell almost with certainty where he will
catch a trout. At this season, feeding trout are to
be found in places which a novice would pass over
as not worth fishing. The strong deep runs are by

no means to be neglected, but the best trout are to
be got in shallow water, at the edges of strong runs,
where they lie, basking in the sun, and on anything
disturbing them run into the current for shelter.
They are also to be found in eddies behind stones,
below banks and tufts of grass; in short, wherever
they can lie unseen and watch for their prey as it
comes down stream. Sometimes also, particularly
if the day is sunny, they will be found in thin quiet
streams, and every run of water detached from the
main current should be fished with great care. The
best of all casts, however, are those where the river
runs beneath the bank. When the waters continue
small and clear for any length of time, the large
trout become alarmed and seek for shelter, and it is
in such places they are to be found.

In a stretch of thin, quiet, exposed water, you
may depend upon every projecting piece of bank
and every large stone sheltering a trout; and if
there is a breeze you have every chance of securing
some of them. The worm should be thrown about
two yards above the place, and allowed to come
down past it, if there is sufficient stream to carry
it; if not, it should be drawn gently down. A
stoppage of the line opposite the place will indicate
the expected event. In large rivers we have fished
with great success those places where the water is
rapid but not very rough, between a pool and a very
strong stream. Streams in the immediate neighbourhood of large pools will generally be found the

best, as the trout come from the pools into the streams to feed.

At some periods of the day trout will not take so readily as at others, and there are times when they seem to leave off altogether, and will take nothing. The angler will generally find that, whatever he is fishing with, trout take most freely during what is usually called the time of the take, which generally happens in the early part of the day, and may be known by seeing the trout rising in numbers. It is evidently then that they are feeding, and they will take almost anything, but they leave off very suddenly, and we have been catching at the rate of three dozen trout an hour with the worm, when all at once, in the very best part of the water, they ceased taking our bait, and also rising at the natural insect, and for the next half-hour we hardly stirred a fin. After a time of almost total stoppage, they will resume again, but not so freely as before.

A showery day with occasional sunshine, or an altogether sunny one without a cloud, is most favourable, but an entirely wet day is also very good. Very good sport may be had in calm thundery weather, even with .   ’   .   . " white clouds " in the sky, as also in blowy wet weather; but good sport is rarely to be met with on a dark windy day without rain, and the worst of all is a bright sky with a few clouds, and strong west wind. In such a day, early morning is the best time. A clear cloudless sky generally indicates a degree of frost in the atmosphere; and when this is the case, the trout do not take readily in the morning, until the heat of the sun begins to be felt. During the months of June and July we have frequently found that we could depend more upon sport when the wind was east than when it was west.

As July draws to a close, trout do not take the worm so well—they begin to be capricious, and will sometimes take only for an hour or two in the forenoon; so that worm-fishing in our earlier streams may be said to be at an end; and if the angler continues it through August, he must have recourse to the more backward districts; and sometimes even to hill-burns. We have known excellent worm-fishers unable to capture a dozen trout in the end of August, where a month earlier they could with ease have filled a basket. And worm-fishing may be limited to six weeks or two months in summer— the time varying according to the season, for which the best guide we can give the angler is, that it generally commences about a week after the May-flies are done, and in streams where these flies do not exist about the beginning of June.

All we have yet said on this head has applied *exclusively* to fishing when the waters are small and clear, and we shall now proceed to what remains of the subject—namely, angling with the worm in flooded waters and hill-burns.

To commence, then, with flooded waters. If the water is very heavy, one or two No. 3 split shot will be found an advantage. In such circumstances we generally use two common bait-hooks, and tie the one about two feet above the other— placing the shot between them about eight inches above the first hook. When the waters are very thick, worms will generally be found most enticing if newly taken from the earth, as in such circumstances trout are guided to them more by scent than sight, and a newly-dug worm has a much stronger smell than a long-kept one.

The parts of the stream where sport may be expected in flooded waters are quite different from those which have been indicated as being suitable when the waters are reduced. Whenever a river begins to flood, trout seek the shallow sides of pools, and the thin and comparatively quiet water at the tails of streams, and in these places they will take the worm readily, until the river gets very large and thick, when they do not take readily, and lie in the eddies a few feet from the edge, keeping as much as possible out of reach of the current. The time when the particles of mud in the water begin to settle, and the water is of a brown colour, is the best of any. The trout now begin to move a little further out, but are still in the moderately quiet water, and here the angler must still look for them.

There is no occasion for fishing up in a flooded water; the thickness of the water prevents the trout from seeing the angler; and the best plan is to commence at the top of a pool or stream, keeping on the shallow side, and throwing in your bait, follow it down to the foot, when you may repeat the process, or seek for some other place. If you are fishing the edge of a pool, where you know there are plenty of trout, you should keep at it for some time, particularly if the river is a large one. In a full flood there are not many places suitable for fishing, and the angler will frequently find that, if he starts at a good place, he will gain nothing by shifting his quarters.

When the river becomes of a dark porter colour, it is better to put off the sinkers, and fish up stream ; and several excellent worm-fishers never use sinkers at all. But when the rivers are very thick, we think the advantages of sinkers considerably exceed the disadvantages, as without them the trout, which are guided to the bait by smell, would seldom see it at all, or if they did, it might be swept away before they had time to seize it.

In flooded waters trout may be captured with worm during the whole angling season, but more readily in June and July than in any of the other months. And if in either of these months there is a long tract of dry weather, and a small flood follows it, an immense quantity of trout may be caught, as after their long fast they will take with the greatest avidity. When the rivers continue small for a long time, the large trout get alarmed, and hide themselves below stones and banks, from which they do not stir, at least in the day-time.

A flood, however, sets them all astir again, and more large trout may then be captured than in any other condition of the water, which is a considerable inducement, notwithstanding the coarseness of the practice, to try it occasionally. When several floods occur in succession about the month of July, trout become gorged with worms, and do not take at all readily, either during the time of the flood, or even when the waters are once more in bait-fishing order—small and clear ; apparently they get enough of worms to satisfy them for the season. In flooded waters, the morning will generally be found the best time, unless in the early part of the season, when the heat of the day is always favourable.

Fishing with the worm in hill-burns, like fishing in flooded waters, is not a very attractive sport, and requires but little of the skill necessary for successful worm-fishing in rivers and waters when they are small and clear. If the banks of the burn are open—that is to say, if it runs over a stony channel—the best way is to use a short rod and fish up in the usual manner. But if, as is frequently the case, the banks almost meet over the burn, the only plan is to drop the worm in and follow it down. There is no danger of the trout seeing you, as in such circumstances they are always under the banks. Every place where there is water to cover a trout should be fished, and we have seen trout nearly half-a-pound weight caught in burns little larger than a sheep-drain, but they are invariably ugly, black, and ill-conditioned, and not worth the trouble of carrying home.   Burns may be fished most successfully after rain ; and as they are generally in late districts, August will be found the best month, but some sport may be had the whole season through, as the trout are invariably hungry.

CHAPTER VIII.

HERE are two flies to which the term May-fly is applied. The first, which is known by anglers generally as the May-fly, is the green drake, a large yellowish fly, which makes its appearance on some streams in great numbers, from the middle to the end of June. Trout are very fond of them, seizing greedily every unlucky individual that ventures on the water; and a couple of them put on a small hook, and allowed to play on the surface will be found very effective, particularly in woody places. It is subject, however, to the great objection of being almost as difficult to catch as the trout themselves; so that as far as angling, at least in Scotland, is concerned, it hardly deserves attention.

The second fly, which is known on Tweedside and in the Border districts as the May-fly, is the phryganea or stone-fly of naturalists; and when we speak of May-fly in the subsequent parts of this chapter or volume, it is this fly to which we allude. Away from Tweedside, its virtues as a lure for trout are little known, and we believe there are numbers of anglers who have never heard of it, and a still greater number who would not know it if they saw it. Unfortunately for the angler, the period of its duration in its matured state is short, but while it lasts it is a most deadly bait for trout; and, under circumstances favourable to its use, a greater weight can be taken by it than by fly, worm, or minnow. The trout captured by it are also larger than those caught by any other means, and in point of condition they are the very finest the river contains; indeed, with this bait, the angler will never get an ill-conditioned fish.

Mr. Wilson, in the *Encyclopædia Britannica*, and again in the *Rod and Gun*, states that the stone-fly comes out of the caddis or case-worm; an aquatic larva, which is to be found plentifully in the bottom of most rivers, enclosed in a curious shell made of sticks and gravel cemented together. But we believe this distinguished naturalist to be in error; the caddis worms, or cod-bait, as they are usually denominated, are to be found in abundance up to the beginning of August, long after the last May-fly has disappeared, and are the larvæ of flies which assume the winged state during that month. In another part of his volume, Mr. Wilson alludes to the creeper or water-cricket as a bait deserving the attention of the angler; this is the stone or

May-fly in its embryo state, and a very deadly bait it is.

Creepers are to be found in the rivers all winter, but it is not till April that they merit the attention of the angler. They then vary in length from three-quarters to an inch and a quarter, are covered with a thin brown shell mottled yellow and black, have numerous legs, and are upon the whole the most venomous-looking insects that the angler in pursuit of his vocation encounters. They are to be found plentifully about the shallow parts of the water under stones, but run so quickly, that it requires some dexterity to catch them, as, unless the water is quite still, it is difficult to see them distinctly. About the middle of May, the time varying according to the season, the creeper leaves the water, where it has hitherto had its dwelling, and crawls on the dry stones, where it casts its shell, and assumes the winged state. The cast-off shells may be seen on the dry channel in great numbers ; and by turning over the stones in such places, the flies may be had in abundance. The full-grown flies are generally about an inch long, and have large wings, which lie flat on the back, but seem of little use, as they invariably trust to their legs for safety. They are of a brownish colour, with a yellow tinge on the belly, and the wings are veined and almost transparent.

Whether the angler intends using the creeper or the fly, he should collect a sufficient number the night before he expects to use them. They are

better newly gathered ; but when the angler is fishing, unless he has an attendant, the gathering of
them consumes much valuable time. The most
convenient method of taking them to the water-side
is in a tin case, shaped something like a powder-
flask. It should be commodious, six or seven inches
long by four or five wide, and an inch and a half
thick. The end at which the flies are to be put in
and taken out should be narrow, with an opening
just sufficient to allow one or two flies to come out
at a time, otherwise the 'angler will have great
difficulty in keeping them in. The lid should be
fastened with a hinge, and the whole canister per-
forated with holes to admit the air. The creepers
can be best preserved in a little of the river-
water, and seem amphibious, as they will live a
whole day in a canister in the angler's pocket. It
is different with the flies ; care must be taken to
keep them dry, as water kills them.

Creepers, then, first merit the attention of the
angler, and may be used with success as soon as
trout come into condition. The rod and tackle
used for worm-fishing will answer very well for this
also, with the exception of the hook ; and with
regard to it, some anglers bait both the creeper and
the fly on an ordinary-sized bait-hook. We however, think two hooks are best, and for creeper-
fishing, use two No. 7 or 8 hooks tied with yellow
silk to the same piece of gut, so close, that the barb
of the one may be about half-an-inch distant from

the barb of the other. Selecting a middle-sized creeper — the best are not the largest, but the yellowest—take the lower hook and put it through the creeper crossways a little above the tail, then take the upper hook, and put it through about the shoulder, according as the size of the creeper suits the tackle. Two hooks possess this advantage over one, that the second hook prevents the creeper from slipping down on the shank of the hook, which, when one hook is used, it always does. In large rivers such as Tweed, or rivers inhabited by large trout, it may be advisable to use two creepers, in which case they should be baited in the same manner, and upon the same tackle as will subsequently be recommended for the May-fly. The creeper should be used in the same manner as a worm—fishing up stream without a sinker, and in the same kind of water, which as we have fully described in worm-fishing it is unnecessary to repeat here. The only difference is, that whereas the angler will frequently catch trout with the worm in moderately still water, he will scarcely ever catch one with the creeper, and should therefore confine his operations entirely to strong water. The state of water and weather most suitable is exactly the same as that looked upon with most favour by the worm-fisher—a small clear water and a sunny day, with a breeze. The best time of day entirely depends upon the weather ; if the weather is mild, trout will take readily early in the morning, but in cold weather they do not commence till 8 or 9 A. M. and leave off in about five or six hours.

The creeper in general will not be found effective until trout are thoroughly in condition, as, until they are so, they have not strength to lie in the streams, where alone this bait is of any use. The longer they remain on the water, the more readily trout take them. They are a much more deadly bait in the middle of May than in the middle of April, and when they are changing into flies, we have found it quite immaterial whether we used the creeper or the fly.

The May-fly is even a more deadly bait than the creeper; but unfortunately the period of its duration is shorter. If the flies can be got of sufficient size, they may be baited in the same manner as the creeper, if intended to be used among small trout when the streams are clear; but in any other circumstances two should be used; and they should be baited in the following manner, substituting for the lower hook of the creeper tackle a larger hook, say a No. 5 or 6 :—Take a good-sized fly, and, entering the large hook about the middle, run it along the body, and bring it out at the tail; then run the fly up the shank of the large hook, and insert the small hook through its shoulders, which will keep it in position; next take another fly, and, entering the large hook a little above the middle, bring it out a little below. If two flies do not cover the hooks properly, the angler should put

M

on three. They are very tender, and must be used
with great delicacy, as the least jerk in casting will
break them; and if the angler strikes, he will
require to bait anew, as the mere drawing through
the water mutilates them.

The flies float upon the surface of the water, so
that they cannot be used exactly like a bait, but
are used in a similar manner. Casting them up
from him, the angler should allow them to come
down a short distance, and then cast again further
up. If the flies are coming down with their wings
out of the water, the trout make a fair rise at them,
but, what is rather singular, and quite unaccountable,
rarely take a proper hold. It is better to have the
flies thoroughly soaked and under the surface, when
the trout take them in a much more deadly manner;
and the first indication the angler sometimes receives
is a stoppage of the line, when he should slacken
for a moment or two; then strike down stream, and
be very careful in landing, as the fish thus taken
are always large and strong.

If the water is clear, the angler should fish in
the same places as with the creeper, with this
difference, that he will meet with success in the
streamy portions of pools, casting up stream to
within half-a-foot of the deep edge. The best casts,
however, in any condition of water, are where the
stream runs below the bank. There trout may be
depended upon, if the angler casts to within a foot
of the edge; and as the current is not so strong at

the edge as a foot further out, the angler must endeavour to keep his line out of the main current, or his flies will come down too fast. Unlike the creeper, the May-fly is most killing when the waters are large and dark-coloured, and must then be used close to the edges; the angler will seldom get a trout in the centre of the current. The deep and strong sides of pools and streams, within a foot of the edge, are the best places; but every spot where a tuft of grass or projecting bush or bank affords shelter to a trout should be fished with great care. A rapid sweep of water past some dry channel can always be relied upon, as the channel produces flies in abundance, and some trout are sure to be on the outlook for them. Greater nicety in casting is requisite in using this bait than any other, as if the angler casts half-a-foot too far out, when the waters are flooded, his labour will be in vain. When the waters are clear, trout will occasionally take in the centre of the stream; but the edges are always mostly to be depended upon, as the trout wishing to feed upon the May-flies come to the edges to look for them.

Trout generally take May-fly best early in the morning; but if much dew has fallen during the night, they will not take freely until the sun has dried it up. There are usually two distinct takes with this bait; one in the morning, from about three to six, when they stop for a short time, but resume again in an hour or two, and continue taking for four or five hours. They take again in the evening, but not so readily. A bright sunny day, with a breeze, or a thoroughly wet one, we consider most favourable.

Trout take the May-fly most readily when it has been about a week on the water; and should a small flood occur, they will take voraciously. If a heavy flood occurs when the flies are all out, it will carry them away, and finish May-fly fishing for the season. The beginning of June is generally the time when this fishing is at its prime; about the middle of the month, or even sooner, the flies get scarce, and the angler must, with great regret, have recourse to something else. For the time it lasts, it is splendid sport. The trout are of large size, and, being in prime condition, run most vigorously, and test to the utmost both the angler's skill and tackle. There are some rivers where the flies are not to be had; and unless there are plenty of stones, they are never found in great numbers; but where they are, trout take them in any size of water, from Tweed to the smallest hill-burn.

Cod-bait, maggots, and the larvæ of some other insects, are very much esteemed by some anglers as baits for trout; but for our own part, we have always found a clear red worm more effective. It is also more easily got, and certainly more agreeable to handle.

CHAPTER IX.

THIS is a very inviting branch of the art. No method of trout-fishing exercises a more lively influence over the angler's hopes and fears, or requires the exercise of so much presence of mind, as trouting with the minnow or parr-tail; a large trout makes a glorious rush at a minnow, and it requires both skill and coolness in order to secure it. Like other methods of angling, minnow-fishing in discoloured water is comparatively easy, and in such circumstances it is better understood by those who practise it than any other branch of the art ; but when the streams are clear, to fish successfully with the minnow, particularly in small waters, requires great dexterity, and is one of the most difficult operations of angling.

One great inducement to use the minnow is the large size of the trout captured. The largest trout taken by the rod are usually caught with it, but the average is not equal in size and still less in condition to those captured with the May-fly. Trout accustomed to prey upon their neighbours usually attain great size, and may be more readily taken by the minnow than by any other means; but these overgrown specimens are generally not inviting.

The value of the minnow, however, as a lure for trout, is to some extent lessened by the difficulty of procuring them. In places and circumstances most favourable to their use, it is sometimes impossible to get them, and we have frequently found the capture of minnows much more difficult than the capture of the trout when we had got them; their capture, therefore, becomes an object of primary consideration.

Minnows are not easily caught till April, as it is not till the streams are in some measure reduced that they venture out from under the banks and other places where they have sheltered themselves from the torrents of winter. In most of the streams in the south of Scotland they are to be found in abundance from April to November. They frequent the thin edges of pools, and every place where a turn of the river leaves a corner, or as it is called "back water," where they can swim unmolested; and in a sunny day such places may be seen almost black with them.

A great many different contrivances are employed to capture them. The small pout or landing-net may be used very effectively during the time of a flood, and it should be worked with the current about the edges of places which the minnows are known to frequent, and in back water. It may also

be employed when a shoal of minnows is found in
some detached piece of water ; in which case the
mud should be stirred up before commencing, when
they may be captured with great ease.

When a shoal of minnows is in a corner they
may be captured without much difficulty.   The
small hoop-net will secure a good many, but a much
more efficient plan is to have a net tied between two
sticks, about two feet separate, with the lower end
of the net leaded.   This is wrought quickly up into
the corner, and as it lies close to the bottom, very
few minnows escape.   By this means as many minnows may be taken at a single haul as will last a
week.   This is the only kind of net we carry with
us when angling, as it goes into little bulk, and a
couple of sticks with which to use it can be picked
up at the water-side.

The great difficulty, however, lies in catching
minnows when they are in the open stream.   For
this purpose we use an oblong net, about two yards
wide and as many long.   This should be attached
to two sticks, with the lower side of the net leaded,
and a few corks put on the upper side, so as to get
as much opening as possible.   The angler should
then place it at the side of some stream where the
minnows are, and chase them into it.   This is the
most reliable of all the methods of capturing minnows.   A net of the size just mentioned, with the
mesh sufficiently small, would cost several pounds ;
but a piece of light canvas, which will do equally

well, and of which we make all our nets, may be
got from any seedsman for a mere trifle.

A very ingenious method of capturing minnows
is practised by anglers in Aberdeenshire, but whether
or not our northern friends can claim the merit of
the invention we cannot say.   It consists of a clear
glass bottle of the structure indicated in the accompanying illustration.

It is used in this way:—A piece of open canvas, or,
what is preferable, small-meshed net, is tied over the
mouth, and a few crumbs of bread put into the
interior.   The bottle is then placed in some stream
which the minnows frequent, with the mouth to
the stream.   The water rushing in agitates the
crumbs and so attracts the minnows, which collect
about the bottom of the bottle, and being naturally
of an inquiring turn of mind, gradually find their
way up to the opening at a, where they enter, and,
fascinated by the all-powerful attractions of the bottle,
remain, and in a few minutes there will be two or
three dozen in the interior.   The objections to the
use of the bottle are of course that it is very incon-
venient to carry, and·very liable to be broken ; but
anglers cannot have everything just to their mind,
and anything is better than running short of minnows ; and when any difficulty occurs in this respect

we would counsel an immediate application to the bottle. We have started to fish with minnow in the early morning without a minnow in our box. Arrived at the water-side we set our bottle, and then put up our rod; by the time this was done the bottle had secured a dozen, which we commenced fishing with, and, then set the bottle again. Now this is very convenient, and wastes less time than any other method of catching minnows, and for the minnow-fisher the bottle is a great invention.

When minnows are intended to be used immediately, they may be captured with a small hook. The best way of doing this is to take a hook, and attach to its shank three or four small pieces of gut, with a pair of small hooks, say No. 11, attached to each, which should hang from an inch to an inch and a half below the single hook. This latter is then baited with a small piece of red worm ; and when the minnows are clustered about it, it is pulled out with a jerk, and the angler will generally get two or three minnows hooked by the outside of the body. The object of this is to get small minnows, as the bait is usually seized by the large ones, to the exclusion of those which the angler wishes to capture.

Those anglers who have the command of a piece of water can always keep a supply of live minnows by enclosing them in a wire box, which should be sunk to the bottom of the water by a weight, and raised when the minnows are wanted. But as

numbers of anglers do not reside at the water-side,
and when engaged in a day's trouting cannot afford
to spend half of it in catching minnows, they should
always be provided with a plentiful supply of salted
ones, which will be found much more deadly than
the best imitations that ever were made. As minnows shrivel up considerably when salted, a size
larger should be selected for this purpose than those
intended to be used fresh. If meant to be used
within four or five days, they should be put in the
strongest pickle, and they will be almost as good as
fresh ; but if not used in a few days, they become
soft and quite useless. For keeping they should be
placed in a jar, with layers of salt between them,
and the brine poured off as it accumulates.

The great objections to salted minnows are, that
they dry into mere skins, so that it is exceedingly
difficult to get them to spin properly ; and that they
are very tender, requiring great care in using, and
even with the greatest care they will not last long ;
and the angler, if possible, should always be provided with a plentiful supply of live ones, as they
are undoubtedly the best. For containing them
when angling there is nothing better than an oblong
tin box (the invention of a very ingenious angler,
the late Mr. Darling of Edinburgh), which can be
strapped round the waist, and is so constructed that
the shaking of the box does not spill the water.
Five or six dozen minnows may be kept alive in
one of them for a whole day by changing the water

occasionally. Those that die should be allowed to remain in the water, as they will keep fresher and firmer there than elsewhere.

A minnow measuring about an inch and three-quarters, total length, tail inclusive, is the size we prefer for trouting at all seasons ; and small minnows are now most commonly used by all able minnow-fishers. A large trout will take a small minnow as readily as a large one, a middle-sized trout more so, and a small trout, which could not take a large minnow, will take a small one readily. In the spring of the year, before trout come into condition, or in autumn, when they are again out of it, a large minnow may answer ; or even in summer, when the waters are flooded, a middle-sized minnow may prove inviting ; but in streams inhabited by well-fed trout, when they are low and clear, minnows cannot be used too small if they will turn the swivels. A large minnow spins in a clumsy, unsightly manner, very different from the neat turning of a small one. Trout, also, can get hold of a small minnow much more easily than of a large one, and so the angler has a much better chance of hooking them. The whitest and most silvery minnows should always be selected ; those that are of a greenish colour underneath being almost worthless.

For trouting with the minnow the rod should be double-handed, not less than fifteen or sixteen feet ; and in order to throw the minnow with the

additions of swivels and shot properly, it must be
stiff. The reel, line, and casting-line in common
use will answer very well for this also. It is the
common practice to dress minnow-tackle on gut
strong enough to draw out a salmon by main force,
as if the trout, which requires the finest gut to
deceive it when angling with the fly, would seize
a minnow at the end of a rope. The argument
used in favour of this practice is, that it lasts the
longer, as no doubt it does ; but what is the use of
tackle lasting that will not catch ? and the strong
white glittering gut upon which minnow-tackles are
usually tied is quite sufficient, when the waters are
clear, to frighten away three trout out of four.
That the gut used for minnow-tackles must be a
little stronger than that used for flies, is quite true,
but a very little difference will do ; if it is so strong
that the spinning of the minnow does not twist it,
it is all that is necessary.

With regard to the number of hooks of which
the minnow-tackle should consist, great diversity
of opinion exists. Some use only two, while others
use four, five, six, and even seven. We have tried
all varieties, and think that two hooks with a drag
behind will kill more than any other combination ;
and two, or at most three hooks are now most commonly used by those whose opinion is worth having.
There are occasions when, from the trout biting shy,
the angler may raise ten trout, and not secure one.
On such occasions we have found a drag, consisting

of two No. 10 hooks tied back to back, and left to play loose about three inches behind the minnow, very effective. Some anglers put a drag-hook about half-an-inch behind the tail, in expectation of those trout that bite short taking hold of this hook with their mouth, but this rarely happens. The tail of the minnow in spinning describes a considerable circumference, and the drag, being further out, a still greater one; so that, if the trout misses the minnow, there is little chance of its catching the drag. The drag which we advise should be dressed on a separate piece of gut, sufficiently long to keep it at least three inches behind the minnow, and attached to the upper hook of the minnow-tackle by a loop, so that it may be taken off or put on at pleasure. The object of having it so far behind the minnow is to catch, by the outside of the body, those trout which bite shy, or miss the minnow.

In order to test whether the two hooks by themselves, or with the addition of the drag, kill most, we fished for several days, time about with each—having the drag on one half-hour and off the next. We have, unfortunately, lost our notes on the subject, but the result was decidedly in favour of a drag. Sometimes more than half of what we caught were taken by it; at others not more than a third. When the drag was on, we did not catch so many trout on the minnow-tackle itself, as when the drag was off, which we account for in two ways. Firstly, the drag is likely to alarm a few trout which would

otherwise take the minnow; and secondly and
mainly, the drag captured at the first rise numbers
of trout which would have repeated their attack
and been caught by the minnow-tackle proper.   On
no occasion did we catch more without the drag
than with it, but we think it quite possible, that in
very clear water, and among very wary trout, the
drag might alarm them; and that if it is not catching a fair proportion—say at least one in four—it
may safely be dispensed with.

The following illustration shows the minnow-
tackle, and also a view of the minnow when baited.

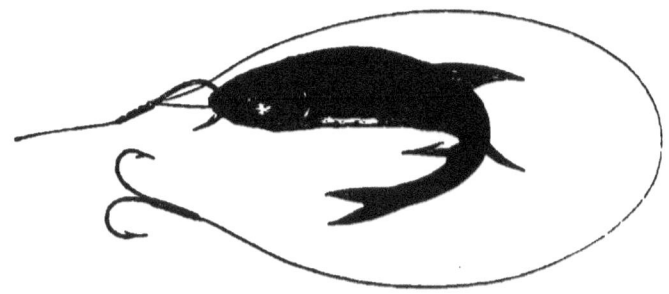

In baiting, take the large hook, and, entering it
at the mouth of the minnow, run it right through
the body, and bring it out about a quarter of an
inch from the tail, leaving the minnow as nearly as
possible in the curve represented in the foregoing
figure.   The object of having the minnow in a
curved form, is that it may turn round when it is
drawn against the stream, and this can be better
accomplished by a small curvature than a large one.
If the body of the minnow is almost doubled up,

the spinning is horrible to behold, and much more
likely to alarm than attract a trout ; the smallest
curvature will do, and the hook should protrude
freely.   The upper hook is then stuck through the
lips, which completes the process, and the angler
should, before commencing, draw it through the
water, to see that it spins properly.

Some anglers use a much larger hook for the
lips than we have indicated ; acting upon the prevalent opinion that trout invariably seize and swallow their prey head-foremost, and that there should
therefore be a large hook there.   So far as our experience goes, this opinion is incorrect.   We have
frequently caught trout with numbers of minnows
and other small fish in their inside, nine out of ten
of which were swallowed tail-foremost ; and this is
only natural, as it is hardly to be supposed that a
minnow will look a trout in the face till the latter
swallows him ; and it is equally improbable that the
trout will let the minnow out of his mouth when
once in, merely for the gratification of bolting him
head-foremost.   From observations taken when the
water was clear, we think that five trout of six seize
the minnow from behind.   We have watched them
come out from below the opposite bank, and follow
the minnow across, always keeping below it, apparently afraid that they might be seen by their
prey, and frequently making no attempt to seize it,
till it was just at the edge.   Some anglers say that
the upper hook is the most deadly, but we have

never found this to be the case, generally capturing four trout on the lower hook for one on the upper ; and even when caught with the upper wire, the appearance frequently shows that they have had the whole minnow in their mouth, and that the upper hook had first come in contact with their mouth in striking, but that the lower hook and the minnow had been expelled subsequently to their being hooked. A large hook through the lips is very easily seen, and also interferes with the spinning of the minnow.

Swivels are a necessary addition to the minnow-tackle, in order to prevent the spinning of the minnow from twisting the line. One should be placed about two feet above the hook, and a second about a yard further up. Split shot, Nos. 2 and 3, are also necessary to the minnow-fisher, and should be placed above the first swivel. Some place them below, but in this position they interfere very much with the spinning of the minnow, as it has to turn round two or three split shot, which, unless a large minnow, it cannot do properly.

Minnow-fishing in flooded waters is so different from minnow-fishing when the waters are clear, that we shall treat of them separately, and shall commence with the flooded waters. The mode of fishing usually adopted is to throw the minnow across the stream, and work it gradually round, now pulling it up the water for a foot or so, and then letting it fall back again, and so on, till it comes round to the side on which the angler is standing. It should be subjected to every variety of motion, one cast drawn steadily against the stream, and the next with short jerks across it ; and even allowing it to go with the current will sometimes prove inviting. Great care should be taken not to lift the minnow out of the water till it is quite close to the edge, as trout will frequently follow the minnow, and make no attempt to seize it until it is just at the edge, when, apparently afraid that their prey is about to escape, they make a rush at it. When a trout has taken the minnow the line should be slackened for a moment or two, to allow it to get the minnow fairly in its mouth, and then the angler should strike firmly. Fly-fishers are exceedingly apt to strike the moment they feel or see anything, which is much too soon. For this reason also a moderately long line is advantageous, as with it the angler cannot strike so soon, and as he is fishing down stream it has also the advantage of keeping him out of sight.

The time of a flood when trout take the minnow most readily is when the water is just beginning to rise, and is of a whitish colour. Then it is that the large trout begin to bestir themselves, and leave the banks and stones where they have been hiding, when the waters were clear, to roam about the sides of pools and the tails of streams ; and here it is that the angler should look for them. When the river is in full flood little can be done, but on its beginning to subside, when the particles of mud are settling, but the water is not yet of the dark porter colour, trout will again take the minnow readily, and in the same places—the ebb sides of pools, and tails of streams. When the waters are in this state, large trout may sometimes be seen rising at the fly close to the edge, on the deep side of the water ; in such circumstances they will take a minnow readily. Sufficient shot should be used when the streams are swollen to keep the minnows well under water, as by doing so it is more likely to be seen, and the light being less the character of the lure is not so easily detected.

In flooded waters trout take the minnow during the whole of the angling season, but more readily in May, June, and July, than in any other months. In May the forenoon is the best time, but in June and July, if the weather is mild, the morning from three to eight is usually the best time ; but if the weather is stormy, trout will take most readily during the day. A flooded water during June or July is a sure index of sport, and should be attended to.

Trouting with the minnow when the waters are clear is a much more difficult and elegant practice than that just described. If the water is sufficiently deep to admit of it, the minnow should be kept well sunk, as it spins better ; and as the angler cannot see the trout take it, he is therefore less likely to strike too soon. In large streams, the necks of pools, rapid broken water of no great depth, detached currents, and the comparatively smooth but strong water at the foot of pools, are in general the best places. Unless the trout are taking very readily, we have never met with much sport in deep water of any kind.

In small streams, when they are clear, it is better to dispense with sinkers, as they make a great splash on alighting, and in shallow water are exceedingly apt to drag the minnow to the bottom. In small streams the main current and strong runs at pool-heads are likely places, but the best casts of all are where the stream runs beneath the bank, even though the water is comparatively quiet. The angler should throw his minnow upon the opposite bank, and drawing it gently off, spin it past the place where he expects the trout is lying, and across to his own side of the water. He may frequently observe the trout come out from the opposite bank, and again and again make a dart at the minnow, and turn back; if he gives his minnow a jerk, which it requires considerable practice to refrain from doing, ten chances to one but he alarms the trout; he should continue playing his minnow in the same manner, and never lift it till it is close to the edge. He must also avoid moving, as the trout, having started from some place where it could not see him, follows the minnow till it comes within sight of him; so long, however, as he remains stationary there is nothing to alarm it, but if he makes any movement it will bolt off immediately.

Even in shallow still water, if there is any projecting piece of bank which can afford shelter to a
trout, the angler may capture it if there is the least
ripple on the water, but such casts require to be
fished very carefully and without a sinker.   In
rivers much fished with the minnow we frequently
get most trout in these out-of-the-way places, as
most anglers pass them over as unworthy of notice.

In small streams, when they are clear and low,
we have fished up stream with minnow with great
success.   All still and even moderately-quiet waters
can be fished just as easily up stream as down, and
by adopting this method, using fine tackle without
a drag and small minnows, we have captured trout
in mill-caulds and other places with no stream in
them, when the sun was shining brightly and not a
ripple on the surface. Even in streams, if the angler
throws his minnow partly across and partly up, and
just pulls it towards him, trout will take it readily.
The best sport we ever had was by fishing up stream
with the minnow and worm alternately.

The minnow may also be baited and used in
the same manner as a worm—a small minnow is
best for this method; but we have never met with
much success by using it in this way, and the sport
is not nearly so attractive as ordinary minnow-fishing.

Trout may be captured with minnow, when the
waters are clear, during the whole season, but the
summer quarter is the best.   In the month of May,

trout generally take most readily in the afternoon, from two or three to six, or even later ; but in June and July, the early morning, and the evening from a little before sunset till midnight, and sometimes on till daylight, are the best times. ‚Should, however, the weather be very coarse, it is useless fishing either in the morning or at night, and the trout will take most readily during the early part of the day.

At all seasons, and at all hours, and in all conditions of water—unless, perhaps, in a full flood, when an occasional blink of sunshine is beneficial —we prefer dark weather for trouting with the minnow ; and in June and July the weather can hardly be too coarse.

In warm summer nights the minnow is a very deadly bait, and should be fished with in quiet still water, and about the shallow water at the foot and edges of pools, as trout cruise about among such places all night.

The parr-tail may almost be considered as a substitute for the minnow, and it is a very deadly lure for large trout in large rivers, particularly when they are flooded, but in small streams we have never found it of much use. It is unnecessary to instruct the reader in the method of capturing parr ; in Tweed, or any other stream where they are numerous, he will generally get far more than he wishes. They frequent the thin water, and take most readily in a sunny day.

The tackle used for parr-tail should be of the same kind as that used for minnow, but with larger hooks, say a No. 1 for the lower hook, and a No. 5 for the upper, with a drag attached as in a minnow-tackle.

The following illustration shows the most approved method of cutting and baiting the parr.

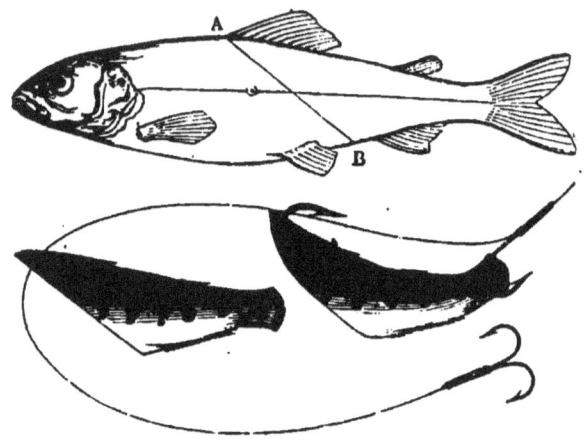

Divide the parr across from A to B, and cut off all the fins till it resembles the second figure, then take the large hook, and entering it at the tail run it along the back and out at the other end, curving the bait to make it spin.

Some anglers bait the parr-tail in the reverse manner from what we have indicated, thinking it is more natural-looking, but when so put on it rarely spins well, and never lasts long; whereas, baited with the small end to the line, it will spin for hours. A parr-tail, bait it any way you please, resembles nothing in life ; and the only object to be aimed at is, as in minnow-fishing, by rapid spinning to conceal the tackle and create an appearance of life.

Thus baited, it should be used in the same manner as a minnow, and among casts of the same description.   The two conditions of water most favourable for the use of minnow are also those most favourable for the use of parr-tail, either when the waters are swollen, or when they are small and clear. Sometimes trout will take minnow more readily than parr-tail, and sometimes, we are informed, though we have never experienced it, they will take parr-tail more readily than minnow ; but for our own part we never use parr-tail when we can get minnows.

CHAPTER X. ·

NGLING in lochs is not held in such estimation as angling in running water. There is a tiresome monotony in fishing continually in still water, where the angler must ply his lure unremittingly in the same manner. There is no whirling eddy, no rippling stream, no projecting bush or bank, where, if the angler casts neatly, he is almost sure to be rewarded for his skill ; the nicety in casting, so essential in order to fish a river successfully, being here almost entirely dispensed with. Nor is there much room for bringing into play knowledge of the habits of the trout, local knowledge almost entirely superseding it ; for the angler, guided by a boatman who is familiar with every bay or bank where sport may be expected, has merely to throw his line, and the only skill requisite is in striking and landing a trout. Fishing from ·the bank, if the angler is without attendant, requires more knowledge of the habits of the trout than fishing from a boat, as the angler has to find out for himself the places in which to fish ; but with all his skill, he can never tell with any certainty which is a good bay and which a bad one, nor can he tell, as in a river, at what cast to expect a trout.

The trout also, from a variety of causes, are not so wary or difficult of capture as the wily inhabitants of most streams. Highland lochs are generally of a dark colour, which helps to disguise the angler's tackle ; and as the trout are little fished for, and rarely disturbed, they are by no means shy.

All these things render loch-fishing a less difficult, and consequently less interesting branch of angling, than fishing in our southern streams. It is indeed the simplest fishing of any, and the one in which the tyro and the accomplished angler are most upon a par ; and we do not wonder that most good anglers prefer capturing smaller but more wary trout in southern streams, to larger and better trout in some remote loch.

Still loch-fishing has its advantages. It is not nearly so fatiguing as river-fishing, and therefore better adapted for some. A sail on a loch possesses great attractions, and as many of our lochs are situated amidst the finest and grandest scenery in the country, the angler must indeed be destitute of taste if he can find no enjoyment in it. In an angling point of view, great inducements to fish in lochs are the large size and fine condition of the trout. In this last respect they certainly surpass those that are found in rivers, being in some lochs quite equal, if not superior, to the salmon itself, and cutting much redder in the flesh.

Most of those acquainted with the subject are of opinion that loch-trout are of the same species as those which are found in rivers, and that their distinctive characteristics are entirely the result of feeding. In some lochs, in addition to the common trout, the *Salmo ferox* is found — a large coarse species, chiefly predatory in its habits, but affording excellent play when hooked. This fish is occasionally caught of great size, and numbers have been caught weighing from ten to twenty pounds. One was caught last year by William Muir, Esq. of Innistrynich, which completely surpasses any that we have ever heard of. This patriarch of the species weighed 39½ pounds, and measured 3 feet 9 inches in length, and 2 feet 2½ inches in girth.

What is remarkably strange, it was taken by Mr. Muir *with fly*, when engaged in angling for salmon in the river Awe where it leaves the loch of the same name, and landed after a run of upwards of two hours, during which Mr. Muir had to cross the river in a boat which fortunately was at hand. What age this fish was it is impossible to conjecture. It was, as its dimensions prove, a well-conditioned fish, and had the curvature of the upper jaw—which is usually considered to betoken age—very strongly developed. Conjecture and imagination would be alike at fault in reckoning what number of lines, of

all descriptions, this monster must have seen in his
time. The amount of learning in such matters which
he must have accumulated during a residence in the
loch of probably not less than fifty years, he put to
a miserable use in the end—selling himself for a
very small mess of pottage indeed, as it was a small
salmon-fly with which Mr. Muir accomplished the
feat. His taking, or rather attempting to take, the
fly at all—as though hooked outside the jaw he rose
at it—can be accounted for on no other supposition
than that old age had weakened his intellect and
impaired his memory. Mr. Muir very properly got
him stuffed.

The common trout in lochs may be captured by
any of the methods usually employed in rivers, but
the only one of these that can be called sport, and
the one that undoubtedly deserves the first notice, is
the artificial fly.

The notion usually entertained, that some particular fly is necessary for every different loch—that
a fly will not take unless its body is made of some
particular dubbing, its wing of some particular feather,
and that the least deviation from rule in the colour
even of the tail-tuft will injure its usefulness—
we believe to be altogether erroneous. The prevailing opinion, that in order to be successful the
artificial fly must be an imitation of some one of the
natural flies on the water at the time, will also,
when applied to loch-fishing, be found absurd. We
should like to know what insects the gaudy-coloured

loch-flies in common use are intended to represent, or what part of the body it is that is imitated by the tinsel so lavishly bestowed? Certainly, we ourselves never saw any insects like artificial loch-flies.

It is quite unnecessary to have a large collection of flies, and the following comprise all that are necessary for any loch in which trout are to be found :—Red, purple, orange, yellow, blue, brown, and green bodies, made either of Berlin wool or mohair, and with or without tinsel. Wings of feathers taken from the jay, woodcock, grouse, teal, or mallard (we prefer the three first mentioned), with black and red cock-hackles, or the small feathers alluded to when treating of river-flies, varied to suit the colour of the fly. A tail is an improvement to the appearance of a good sized fly, and may be made of a few fibres of the feathers taken from · the neck of the golden pheasant, or a tuft of Berlin wool of a different colour from the body of the fly. In loch as in river fishing, the angler must be cautioned against trusting too much in flies.

In dressing loch-flies, the hackle may either be carried down the full length of the body, or confined to the part immediately below the wings ; the latter is perhaps preferable, as it makes a neater and more shapely fly. Commence operations at the bend of the hook—at the place where you intend the tail of the fly to be—by fastening on the tail-tuft, and the end of the thread of worsted or mohair,

of which you are to form the body, also the end of
the thread of tinsel. Then lay the gut along the
shank of the hook, and tie them firmly together until
within five or six turns of the end of the hook, where
fasten on, and divide the wings in the usual way,
seeing that they stand well apart; next fasten on
the hackle, and turn it round frequently, as close
under the wings as possible, giving the silk one or
two turns round it to keep it secure, and cut off
the remainder, as in dressing a small fly. Then take
the thread of worsted, and wrap it firmly round up
to where the hackle is, and give the thread a turn
or two round it. All that now remains to be done
is to wrap the tinsel firmly round the body up to
the place where your silk thread is, which you should
whip three or four times over all, and finish off as
close to the wings as possible. Finishing under
the wings makes a very neat fly, and if well done
it is hardly possible to tell where it is finished.
We do not know if this is the artistic mode of
making a loch-fly, but it is the best way we know,
and the following illustration shows what like they
are when made.

Flies made of the materials already mentioned,
and varied in size according to circumstances, are
all that is necessary for loch-fishing in Scotland.
To adapt the size to the circumstances is, however,
a matter of no small difficulty. The same causes
which regulate the angler in fixing the size of his
river-flies should be his guide here also. The great

point at which to aim is to have a fly sufficiently
large to ensure its being seen, but not large enough
to allow the trout to detect its artificiality.   To

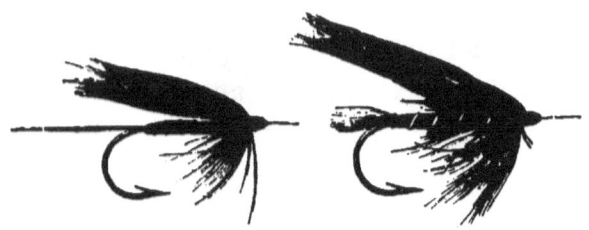

accomplish this the angler who visits a number of
lochs must be provided with all sizes of flies from
No. 10 up to No. 3.

The colour of the water and the amount of wind
are two of the principal causes which should regulate
the angler in selecting the size of fly.   If the water
is dark-coloured, a size or two larger should be used
than when it is clear.   If there is a strong breeze of
wind blowing, a size or two larger may be used than
when there is little wind ; and when there is no
wind at all, we have found an approach to river
sizes, say Nos. 9 and 10, most effective—always
remembering to increase or diminish the size, according as the state of water and wind prevents the fly
being easily seen or the reverse.

We once had a signal proof of what difference
the wind will make, when fishing a loch from a
boat, in company with a friend.   We commenced
with small-sized flies, and our friend with large ones.
The breeze was very gentle when we began, and

while it continued so, we captured six trout for our friend's one ; but after we had been fishing for some time, it began to blow violently, when the tables were turned, leaving us behind. After waiting long enough to ascertain the point, we put on large flies, which put us both on an equal footing. The depth of water also, to a certain extent, regulates the size of fly. The trout in lochs usually lie near the bottom, and if the water is deep it will require a larger size of fly to attract their attention ; but as it is usual for the angler to fish in about the same depth of water, there is no occasion for his troubling himself about this.

The colour of the water and the amount of wind should also, to some extent, regulate the colour of the fly. In dark-coloured lochs, red and the more gaudy colours will be found most enticing, while, in a clear water, brown and the more sober colours will be found best. Also, in a stormy day, a gaudy-coloured fly will answer best ; but in a calm one, always choose the less glaring colours, and avoid tinsel.

The only other cause which should influence the angler in selecting the proper size and colour of flies is the wariness of the trout. Where trout are not at all shy, larger and more gaudy flies may be used than where they are much fished for, or shy from any cause, as a shy fish is very suspicious, and will detect the counterfeit in a smaller fly than another fish will. It is exceedingly difficult to regulate the size and colour of flies by theory, but in practice it is much simpler. Keeping the general principles in mind, the angler should commence with two or three different sizes and several different colours, and when he ascertains which is taking best, regulate accordingly. Just as in river-fishing, it is advisable, if the trout evince a decided preference for one fly, to put on two or three of that description.

The gut upon which loch-flies are dressed, and by which the casts are made up, is in general far too thick. All the fine hanks are selected for river purposes, and the strong white glittering ones set aside for loch-fishing, as if gut could not be got sufficiently thick, and a loch-trout would seize a fly at the end of any thing. It is quite true that stronger gut may be used with success in lochs than in rivers, yet the finer the gut the better the chance of success. In all kinds of angling, it is of the utmost importance to have the connecting link between the lure and the rod as little seen as possible. Their common use of thick gut is one of the reasons why anglers meet with no success when there is no wind, and with but little when there is only a gentle breeze. It is erring on the safe side to use fine gut, and we never yet got a hank of gut which we considered too fine for dressing loch-flies on. In some lochs we have caught more trout than anglers accustomed to fish them every day, simply because we used fine gut, and they used it very thick and white.

The rod for fly-fishing from a boat need not be longer than thirteen or fourteen feet, as that is long enough to keep the angler out of sight, and a very long rod is cumbrous to manage. In angling from the bank, a rod of two feet longer might be advisable, in order to reach the places where the trout lie. The reel should be large enough to contain fifty or sixty yards of line ; for if you get a large fish, you must exhaust it by length of line, since you cannot follow it as on a river. But there is no occasion to have either the line or the triple-gut casting-line thicker than what is used for ordinary trouting purposes. A landing-net is an almost indispensable article when fishing from a boat, and every angler should be provided with one.

The cast of flies should be made up in the usual manner, but as the flies are larger, the distance between them should be increased to about three feet. As to the number of flies to be used at a time, the angler may with safety use as many as he can manage properly ; but we think that in fishing from a boat four will generally be found sufficient, as if there is a great number it is exceedingly difficult to prevent them from hanking below the boat when landing a trout. In fishing from the bank, the angler may use as many flies as he can throw out properly.

The great object in loch, as in river fishing, is to get over the ground quickly and thoroughly, if possible bringing your flies within range of every

O

trout in the water you pass over. And as the first few yards of the flies' course is the most effective, you should cast frequently. When angling from the bank, the flies should be thrown straight out as far as possible, and then drawn gently towards the shore. If allowed to remain still the trout would at once discover the deception, to obviate which, the flies must be always kept in motion ; a slight jerking motion we have generally found most enticing. After the flies have traversed a few yards of water, the angler should cast again a few yards further along, and so on, only casting once in the same place. When angling from a boat, the usual way is to place it with its side to the wind, and allow it to drift down ; the boatman keeping it the requisite distance from the shore. If the breeze is strong, the boat will drift too fast to admit of fishing the water thoroughly, and a large stone attached to a rope should be put out at the windward side to act as a drag. Commencing at the bow of the boat, the angler should first cast straight out, and then go gradually round, casting to leeward, and in a fresh piece of water every time till he come to the stern, when he should begin again.

The parts of the loch in which to fish, as has been before stated, can only be ascertained with certainty by local experience. The amount of food is the principal cause which influences trout in their preference of one part of a loch to another, and this depends entirely upon the nature of the bottom.

The bays and creeks in the immediate vicinity of any place where a stream enters are generally good ground, as the stream brings down mud and vegetable matter, which, being deposited in the neighbourhood, is peculiarly favourable to the development of insect life. It is by no means uncommon to find the trout in one part of a loch quite red in the flesh, and in another quite white, the red-fleshed ones being on a superior feeding-bank. Sport may almost always be depended upon in the neighbourhood of weeds and large stones, which afford shelter to the trout. The angler should allow his boat to drift alongside, and cast as near to the weeds and stones as possible. Places where the water is overhung with trees should also be fished with great care, as some trout are generally on the outlook for any insects that may drop or be blown from them.

The best trout taken with the fly are usually got in from four to ten feet of water. In the deep parts of the loch little can be done, we believe, because there are few trout in them, the aquatic insects on which they feed being mostly found about the edges, where the sun's rays penetrate to the bottom. Even supposing there were plenty of trout in the deep water, unless they should be swimming about near the surface, they could not see the angler's flies ; so that fishing in deep water will never prove remunerative.

The opinion prevails that it is of no use angling

in lochs unless there is a strong breeze ; and if the same size of flies is used always—whether the waters are lashed into foam, or gently agitated, or dead calm—this is quite true. But by adapting the flies and tackle to the circumstances of the case, very good sport may be had when there is the slightest breeze, and something may even be done when there is not a ripple on the water. In a calm, a long rod and line should be used, in order to get the flies as far away from the boat as possible, as the sight and motion of the boat will alarm the trout in the immediate neighbourhood. When there is no breeze, after the flies light they should be allowed to remain where they are until the motion of their falling has subsided, and then drawn by short jerks towards the angler, more rapidly than if there was a breeze of wind. A larger portion of the line should also be kept in the water, and great care taken to make as little disturbance as possible. Perhaps the best way of fishing in a calm is to have the boat slowly propelled by one oar from the stern, making as little disturbance as possible, and throw gently over every trout that rises at the natural fly. Or if the trout are evidently—as they sometimes are—rising in shoals, the boat may be pulled into the centre of the shoal ; and when the alarm caused by the disturbance has subsided and the trout begin to rise again, the angler should drop a small fly lightly on the spot, and he will have a good chance of securing the fish.

The most favourable weather is a day with a

good breeze of west wind, and alternate sunshine
and shower. The trout never take readily, particularly if the air is at all cold, unless the sun is
shining. A wet day is better than a cloudy one
without rain, but not equal to a sunny one. In the
early months east wind will mar the angler's sport,
but in July and August it is not so objectionable ;
since at that season, even with it, the air is generally
sufficiently warm.

The best time of year for fly-fishing depends, as
in rivers, upon the season. If the weather is mild,
trout may be taken readily in May ; but this is
rarely the case, and June and July may be set down
as the best two months of the year. In August the
trout will not rise so readily, but will take again in
September and the beginning of October ; but fly-
fishing in the fall of the season can hardly be called
sport, as the trout do not begin to take, after having
stopped, till they are in declining condition.   ·

The best time of day depends entirely upon the
weather, and it is impossible to name any time with
certainty, as the trout may change their humour
with every change in the sky. In May the forenoon will generally be found the best ; but in June
and July from seven in the morning till noon, and
again the afternoon from three to five, are the most
favourable times. If the weather is very warm, as
it sometimes is in July, and there is no wind, about
sunset, and an hour or two after it, will be found
worth all the rest of the day.

Angling in Loch Leven has come very much
into fashion of late years. For some time it was
supposed, upon what grounds we are not aware,
that the trout of that loch would not rise freely to
the artificial fly. This, however, has been found
a mistake; they rise just as readily as the trout of
any other loch, and there are few lochs so well
stocked, and certainly none that contain trout of finer
quality. We believe that loch contains more trout
for its size than any other loch in Scotland, which is
entirely attributable to the great extent of its feeding-
ground; the greater part of it being of the uniform
depth of from six to twelve feet; just the depth of
water best suited to breeding fish. The fishing is
under the management of a tacksman, who keeps a
number of boats which are let out at half-a-crown
an hour, including a man to manage the boat, and,
considering that the trout sell at eighteenpence a
pound, that two can fish from a boat, and that
anglers are allowed to keep their fish, we think the
charge exceedingly moderate. Any of the flies we
have recommended for loch-fishing will suit Loch
Leven; we have also had very good sport by trolling
with Brown's artificial minnow.

The artificial fly is by far the most agreeable and
sportsmanlike method of capturing trout in lochs,
but is liable to this objection, that the large trout
are very rarely taken by it. And though the reader
may hear of five, six, and even eight pound trout
being taken by this means, he may rest assured

that, however well he may fish, he will catch but few such.

The large trout in-lochs seem to live principally on their smaller neighbours, and can be more readily taken by trolling than by any other means. It is not at all uncommon to find the trout captured with fly rarely exceeding half-a-pound in weight; while trout of five, ten, and sometimes even twenty pounds weight may be taken by means of a small fish for a bait. If the trout are not large, a minnow or parr-tail will form the best bait; but if the angler expects to meet with trout exceeding two or three pounds in weight, a whole parr should be used, and it is superior to a trout, being much more silvery and easily seen. If parr are not procurable, recourse must be had to trout, and if, as is generally the case, they are very dark-coloured when caught, putting them in a white basin and exposing them to the sun will improve their appearance. Where the trout are very large, as in lochs frequented by the *Salmo ferox*, a quarter of a pound trout will not make too large a bait.

The rod for trolling need not be long, but it is absolutely necessary that it should be stiff, as a quantity of line with a heavy fish at the end of it is a severe strain upon a rod, and in such circumstances a supple one would be quite unmanageable. The reel should be large enough to contain at least sixty or seventy yards of good strong line, as a trout of ten or fifteen pounds will make a desperate struggle,

and test severely both the skill of the angler and
the boatman. After the ordinary line there should
be a strong triple-gut casting-line, tapered from the
line to where the trolling-tackle is attached. The
gut on which the hooks are tied should be stronger
than what is used for any other trouting purpose,
and almost as thick as that used for salmon-fishing.
This strong gut is so rarely devoid of a white glossy
appearance, and requires to be stained so dark
before it is divested of it, that we prefer triple-gut
twisted, which can be got very fine, and it is not so
easily seen as a single thread of the same thickness.
If there are pike in the loch it will be necessary to
tie the hooks on gimp, as the teeth of that fish are
very sharp, and will sometimes bite through triple-
gut. Two lengths above the hooks a large swivel
should be placed, and three or four lengths farther
up it is advisable to have a second. Large swivels
are greatly superior to small ones, as they are not so
liable to go wrong, and also act as sinkers. When
sinkers are required, swan-shot should be used,
which may be placed between the swivels, or above
them.

The number of hooks of which trolling-tackles
are composed is very various, and we have seen as
many as seven pairs on one tackle. But it is very
doubtful if any advantage is gained by surrounding
the bait with hooks in this manner, and we think
that three, or if the bait is a large one at most four
pairs will be quite sufficient. The hooks should be

tied with good strong silk to the same piece of gut, regulating the distance between each pair to suit the length of bait to be used. One of the hooks of the lowermost pair should be stuck into the bait a little above the tail, one of the second pair about the middle, and one of the third pair through the lips. One of the hooks of each pair is thus hidden in the fish, and the other left exposed. The bait must be sufficiently curved to make it spin.

Another kind of trolling-tackle is made in the same manner as the common minnow-tackle, but with much larger hooks. The lowermost hook should not be less than from two and a half to three inches long. Fastened to the upper hook is a separate piece of gut, on which are two pairs of hooks, one of which is stuck into the bait about the middle, and the other left loose as a drag, a little beyond the tail. The method of baiting this is the same as that of baiting a minnow, and when the trout or parr is soft from being kept, it has its advantages, as the large hook through the bait keeps it in position.

The best method of trolling is to place the rods in the stern of the boat, with at least twenty yards of line out, so as to keep the bait a good distance from the boat. The latter is then pulled along at a pretty smart pace, and its rising to the waves will play the bait quite as invitingly as the angler could do by hand. A sufficient number of shot should be used to keep the bait two or three feet under the surface, as it is there more likely to attract attention,

and the light being less, the character of the lure is
not so easily discerned.

The notion that the boat must be pulled against
the wind, common among the boatmen, and to which
they adhere so tenaciously, is erroneous; but it would
be difficult to make a Highland boatman believe this.
The error arises from the supposition that the wind
is driving the water in the direction it is blowing,
whereas it is merely the form of the wave that is
going forward, and the bait will spin just as well if
the boat is rowed in any direction which is most
convenient; either directly with the wind or sideways to it. When the wind is very strong, it is
almost impossible to row the boat sufficiently fast
against it to keep the bait spinning.

Trolling should be done in deeper water than
fly-fishing, and every part of the loch may be trolled
over, avoiding the very deep portions. Water from
ten to twenty feet deep is usually considered the
best ground, but stray fish, and those generally of
large size, may be taken even in the middle of the
loch.

A dark stormy day is considered most favourable,
but no day is objectionable, and even in a dead calm
trout may be taken with a small natural or artificial
minnow, when they cannot be taken by any other
means. In the early part of the season trout will
take most freely during the forenoon; but in June
and July, if the weather is at all warm, early morning is the best time, and when there is no wind from

sunrise to sunset is the only time when there is much chance of sport by this means. Large fish are most inclined to take when the waters of the loch are high and dark-coloured after a flood.

Trolling is dull work, as it is by no means uncommon for an angler to toil a whole day without getting a single specimen, and even when successful the merit of the capture lies partly with the boatman, who knows the places and rows the boat. Unless the loch is too stormy to fish with fly, we would never advise any one to devote himself to trolling exclusively, but when on the loch it is as well to be provided with a trolling rod and tackle, and to use it when rowing from one place to another, thus filling up the intervals during which he cannot use the fly.

We now come to the last and least interesting method of capturing trout in lochs—namely, with the worm—and on this point we shall be very brief, as it possesses few attractions.

Angling with the worm can be most successfully practised from the shore, but the angler will require to wade, and a long rod and line are necessary to reach the places where the trout lie. A No. 3 hook is a very good size, and a pretty large black-headed worm should be used. The places frequented by the fly-fisher are also those where the worm-fisher will meet with most sport, and he, like the fly-fisher, is the better of a breeze of wind. After throwing out the worm, it should not be allowed to lie at the bottom, as in that position it is not likely to attract observation, but should be drawn gently along the ground.   The best months are June and July, and the morning is the best time of day.

When any river which enters the loch is in full flood good trout may be captured with the worm. The use of a boat would be advisable, and the angler should row it round immediately outside of the place where the muddy water becomes mixed with that of the loch, and throwing his bait into the stream, allow it to come towards him.   Numbers of good trout may be taken in this way, as they congregate about the mouth of the stream to get the food which it brings down.

CHAPTER XI.

E have treated at considerable length of the four principal methods usually employed for capturing trout. The reader may perhaps be disappointed that salmon-roe fishing has not been added as a fifth ; but our reason for keeping it out is, that we do not consider it a justifiable method ot angling, the high price the roe brings affording great, indeed the principal, encouragement to the wholesale destruction of breeding salmon which goes on in Tweed and its tributaries during close time. We think, that in the first Act introduced upon the subject of the salmon-fisheries, there should be a clause inserted rendering it illegal for any one to fish with salmon-roe, or to be found with it in his possession. Doing away with this traffic would do more to protect the Tweed than all the water-bailiffs between Tweedsmuir and Berwick. There are certainly a few salmon taken shortly before the fishings close, with roe sufficiently matured for curing ; but the roe, legally obtained in this way, is not a hundredth part of that taken illegally during close time. Moreover, the fact of salmon being caught in this state in the open season proves that the rivers are open too long, and that the law should be altered in this respect also.

At certain seasons roe is certainly a murderous bait, and a practised roe-fisher might almost depopulate a stream ; but then it is only deadly in the fall of the year when trout are out of condition, or in the spring before they come into it ; and killing trout in such circumstances deserves no better name than butchery. For some time roe was, and is still to the north of the Forth, considered an infallible specific for catching trout ; a reserve which is to be brought to the attack when everything else fails. It is not, however, looked upon with quite so much favour now. Anglers have begun to find that the presence of a pot of roe in their baskets when setting out by no means ensures the presence of trout there on their return ; and we have seen anglers, starting for a first trial of this wonderful bait, sit down at a pool, and, wrapping their plaids about them, remain there for hours, no doubt expecting, according to the common notion, that they would attract all the trout in the neighbourhood, and quite astonished when they had to return without a single one. The fact is, that the wonderful properties of this bait are greatly exaggerated ; as a lure for trout during the season when they are in condition it has no advantage, in any state of water, over the lures which have been treated of, and in clear water, during the day, it is almost useless. Nor is the sport, if sport it can be called, by any means attractive ; and the practice is so simple as to render it quite unworthy of the attention of the sportsman.

That trout can detect the presence of roe in their neighbourhood is certain ; but, in our opinion, the distance at which it is supposed they can do so is greatly exaggerated.   Mr. Stoddart mentions that on several occasions he captured trout which he had every reason to believe had been attracted for half-a-mile by the scent of this bait, which is certainly giving trout credit for possessing extraordinary powers of smell.   We think that on the occasions alluded to by Mr. Stoddart, he captured the trout which belonged to a part of the river so much below where he was, not because they had been attracted all that distance by the smell of the roe, but because, when a flood begins to subside in the fall of the year, they travel upwards in search of spawning-ground.   As a proof of this let any one commence angling with the roe in a favourable state of the water during March or April, when trout will take it as readily as in November.   On his first commencement at the top of a pool, which we shall suppose is a hundred yards long, he may capture in an hour three or four dozen of trout ; but then there comes a stop, and though he were to fish all day in the same place he would get very few more.   Let him transfer his operations to the foot of the pool, and he may capture as many more, showing either that the trout cannot detect the presence of roe a hundred yards above them, or that they cannot be troubled to go so far for it; and as they take it as readily in April as November, there is no reason why they should not go as far to seek it in the one month as the other. Another point—which the framers of the next bill upon the salmon-fisheries should keep prominently in view—is the protection of the young salmon or parr. During the months of April and May, when they are changing into smelts and migrating to the sea, killing them is an offence liable to heavy fines; but for the rest of the season, the poor silly parr is at the mercy of every boy who can muster twopence to buy gut and hooks; and thousands of them are slaughtered in Tweed every day during summer, and not by boys only, but by grown men pretending to be anglers. If such have not sufficient skill to capture trout, we hope the law will step in to prevent them massacring the innocents in this manner.*

In the first chapter of this volume it was mentioned that there were not three days from May till

---

* Since we wrote the above passage both roe-fishing and killing parr have been made illegal;. but as we believe both are still carried on, if not so openly, nearly as destructively as ever, we have allowed the passage to stand, and hope all honest anglers will set their faces against such a disgraceful infringement, not only of the law, but of fair fishing, and not bring discredit upon the fair fame of the craft.

October in which a good angler should not kill at least twelve pounds weight of trout in any county in the south of Scotland. There are days when he may easily kill twice that quantity, and the angler who, fishing a whole day—that is to say, for nine or ten hours—cannot capture on an average fifteen pounds a-day, has not yet attained to eminence in the art. Most anglers seem to think that the difficulty will be to kill the required quantity when the water is clear, but this is not the case, the difficulty is only when the water is flooded. Sport in clear water is certain ; sport in flooded water is uncertain. There are occasions when the water is flooded that trout take very readily, and when large baskets may be got with little trouble by almost any one ; but these occasions are " like angels' visits, few and far between," and it has not been our lot to fall in with many of them. Indeed, we have frequently, in a dark water, had great difficulty in killing twelve pounds weight, when we could with ease have killed twice that quantity had the water been small and clear ; and all our best takes have been when the water was in that condition. There are some days, however, even in clear water, when the most skilful angler will require to work very hard to get the required quantity. Nor is it at all possible to accomplish it by a continuous use of any one method of angling. The fly-fisher cannot do it ; the worm-fisher cannot do it ; the minnow-fisher cannot do it ; and, as a matter of course, the May-fly fisher cannot do it. It can only be done by a judicious use of the four methods, according to circumstances. Nor can it be done by fishing continually in one stream; the stream also must be varied according to circumstances.

In order to fulfil the promise made to the reader of explaining how this can be done, we shall now go over the whole angling season, and mention the occasions when the angler wishing weight should employ the different methods; but before doing so we shall mention some points which apply equally to all seasons.

One of these is, that large rivers are not so much to be depended upon as small streams, partly because they do not contain so many trout in proportion to their size, and partly because, from unknown causes, the trout in them are more capricious. In the time of a take, large quantities of trout may be caught in them with very little trouble; but at other times the angler will have great difficulty—and will occasionally find it impossible—to kill the required twelve pounds. For this reason, if the angler is not meeting with success in large rivers, he should have recourse to the smaller rivers and waters, and failing these to burns, in which some trout may always be had. We shall suppose that the angler keeps this in view throughout the season, so that it will be unnecessary to make any further allusion to it.

Fishing can be most successfully practised alone; but if the angler fishes in company, he should come to some arrangement with his friend respecting a division of the water before starting, as he who fishes the water first has undoubtedly the best chance. In a large river, and fishing with the fly, it does not make much difference; and even in a small water the trout will rise freely if allowed to remain undisturbed for an hour or so. But it is different in fishing small clear streams with the worm; there the second angler has not nearly so good a chance as his predecessor, and with the minnow or the Mayfly, the first angler would entirely mar the sport of the one following him.

Another point equally suitable to all seasons is, if you have got an unlimited stretch of water to fish, to do so very quickly, only taking the best casts. This is peculiarly applicable when the trout are not taking freely. The secret of success lies, to a considerable extent, in getting over the ground rapidly, and the angler who stands casting repeatedly in a spot when he is getting nothing need never expect to fill his basket.

Before trout come into condition there is no inducement to fish for them; and not being in the streams, no reliance can be placed upon their taking; and as they are rarely in condition all over a county till the first of May, we shall begin with that month. Should trout come into condition sooner, the lures suitable for May will be found suitable for April also.

In the beginning of May it is of little use starting before eight o'clock in the morning, as the weather is generally cold; if the weather is warm, however, trout will take an hour or two earlier. When the waters are clear the angler should commence with the creeper, and continue using it till he sees the take has commenced, when he should at once change to the fly, and make the most of his time. At this season the take lasts longer than at any other, and if the day is favourable the angler may kill the required quantity in a few hours in the forenoon. During the afternoon—that is to say, from two or three o'clock till six or seven—the minnow will frequently be found the best; and a very good plan is to fish up with the creeper and fly, and then back over the same ground with the minnow. If neither the creeper, fly, nor minnow will take, recourse must be had to the worm; but this is rarely the case, and unless on the occasion of a full flood, the angler may never have occasion to use the worm till the end of June. When the waters are in full flood recourse must be had to the worm; and when they are rising, or again falling, from the time that the particles of the mud begin to subside until the waters become of a dark porter colour, the minnow will be found very deadly. The worm and the minnow should be used the whole season through when the waters are in the states just mentioned, but when they become of a dark porter colour the lures appropriate to the season come into play; and in May, in such a case, reliance can always be placed upon the fly.

About the middle of the month the May-fly makes its appearance, and with it the angler will have no difficulty in filling his basket. In streams where the May-fly is not to be had, the angler should use worm and minnow in the morning, and whenever he observes the trout rising at the natural insect, change to the fly. The minnow will again be found effective in the evening. Even in streams where May-flies abound minnow or worm will sometimes take better than they do early in the morning, and if the weather is very dark and stormy, the minnow will frequently be found most effective all day.

When the May-flies have been two or three weeks on the water, or about the middle of June, they are not to be found in such numbers ; the trout also do not take them so readily ; and filling even a twelve-pound basket becomes rather difficult. The trout have given up taking fly readily, and have not yet begun to take worm ; they appear to be resting after the high feeding they have enjoyed for the last six weeks. Loch-fishing being now in its prime, the angler would do well to give it a trial, as he will not lose much by a ten days' absence from the rivers. In these the worm and minnow in the morning, the fly in the forenoon, and the minnow and fly in the evening, will be found the best means of filling a basket ; and in small waters and hill-burns trout will now take the worm readily.

From the middle to the end of June worm-fishing commences, and from this period to the end of July large basketsful of trout may be depended upon, no matter what the state of weather or water. A good arrangement for a day's trouting at this season is to start very early in the morning—the earlier

the better—and fish down a few miles with the
minnow, and then fish back again with the worm ;
or if the angler has not the gift of early rising he
may start about breakfast-time, taking his dinner
with him, and fish up with the worm and down again
with the minnow in the evening. If the weather is
dark and stormy, the minnow will frequently be
found most deadly during the whole day.

About the beginning of August another change
begins to take place in the inclinations of the trout.
Unless the weather is showery, or particularly favourable, they will not take the worm readily ; and frequently only take it for an hour or so in the heat of
the day. There is also a visible falling off in the
size of the trout caught with it—a sure sign with
any kind of fishing that it is approaching a ter-
mination. Nor will the minnow, unless the streams
are swollen, aid the angler in his emergency ; there
is nothing for it but to have recourse to the more
backward districts and smaller waters.

About the end of August trout begin to take
the fly freely, and continue doing so all through
September, and reliance can generally be placed
upon it, particularly in coloured water ; should it
fail, recourse must be had to some hill-burn, where
the worm will always be found effective.

By the beginning of October all the spawning
trout are out of condition ; the small ones, however, which do not spawn, afford very good diver-
sion until far on in the month, by which time
even they are quite unworthy the attention of the

sportsman; affording no play when hooked, and no satisfaction when caught. In other respects also angling is divested of half its charms; there is nothing cheering, nothing invigorating, in a ramble by a river's side. The angler's path is not now adorned with the daisy and the violet, or scented with the perfume of innumerable wild flowers; and the singing of the birds, and the hum of the mountain-bee, are replaced by the sighing of the wind among leafless branches, or along a bleak hill-side. Nature is fast resuming her wintry aspect, and

> " When chill November's surly blast
> Makes fields and forests bare,"

the angler who has followed his vocation in the joyous spring-time, and again when the summer's sun throws his rich glories over mountain and valley, and has continued with undiminished ardour when the breezes play cooler,

> " And Autumn's soberer hues
> Tint the ripe fruit, and gild the waving corn,"

will not lose much by bidding adieu to the streams for the season, and awaiting, with thankfulness for the past, and bright hopes for the future, the coming of another spring.

OPINIONS OF THE PRESS.

BLACKWOOD'S MAGAZINE.

" Mr. Stewart has the reputation of being a most successful angler, and his fame is on many waters. Therefore, holding the views which we have already expressed touching the general selfishness of the fraternity, we cannot too much admire his single-heartedness in compiling a work which, if attended to, must transmute the veriest tyro into a tolerably prosperous fisherman. We suspect that some who now rank as his rivals will barely thank him for his revelations, on the score that it is not expedient either to multiply the number of rods, or to divulge secrets which must tend to a considerable thinning of the streams. They, the adepts, believe themselves to constitute a high and worshipful piscatory lodge, with mysteries peculiar to their degree ; and they may not altogether approve of the extreme liberality of their excellent brother in opening the eyes of the uninitiated. However, they may comfort themselves with the reflection that darkness rather than light is the deliberate choice of the million. The best teaching in the world is thrown away upon stupidity and self-conceit ; and that not only in ethics, but in such practical matters as angling. . . . One special recommendation of this book as an angling treatise is, the clearness with which Mr. Stewart lays down his positions, and the care which he has bestowed on the proof. He does not content himself with merely giving directions ; he explains, and always lucidly, why such directions are given."

ATHENÆUM.

" Although this book be on angling, there is something new in it. We feel bound to say this much at the outset ; for any one might be excused for believing that all that could be written on this subject had been accomplished long ago. Mr. Stewart, how- ever, has given additional value to a pleasant little volume by his expression of some original views and assertions, based upon experience. . . . . For our own parts, we can honestly declare that this little book is really both amusing and instructive —an assertion which we proceed to prove by one or two brief extracts. . . . . We have had regard in our extracts to the amusing passages in *The Practical Angler.* They who require to be told how to be as successful in clear as in dark waters must study the lessons patiently and intelligibly given by a master of more than fifteen years' experience."

ILLUSTRATED LONDON NEWS.

" That patient class of British sportsmen for whom the Blink-bonnys and the Skirmishers of the turf live and race in vain, and whose hearts are not with the Kestrels or the Americas on the waters of the Solent, or in the tents of the scorers at Lord's or Kennington Oval, but continue to believe, summer after summer, in the spirit of the old song—

> ' Oh ! the gallant fisher's life,
> It is the best of any !'

will take this terse little book to their bosom, and make it the companion of many a river-side pilgrimage. Its aim is not to give any highly-tinted dissertation on the joys of angling, or to produce a series of mental pictures of its most favoured haunts. Alas, for the silver trout ! the author had a much more practical and deadly object in view ; and although the gentle craft have had teachers, and to spare, since their quaint old Isaak wrote, it was reserved for him to prove that almost, if not quite, as good sport may be had in clear water as in coloured.

" Mr. Stewart brings a large stock of enthusiasm, and fifteen years' practice, to his work. He has gleaned for his letterpress, and his hook and bait illustrations, from nearly all the first amateurs and professional anglers of the day, and exchanged minds with Jamie Baillie, the veritable senior wrangler of fly-fishing in Scotland. Delightful as it may be to a beginner to wander, rod in hand, along the banks of some river in May or June, among meadows rich with the daisy and the cowslip, or to contemplate nature in her grander, but not less beautiful aspect, on the rocky heather-clad verge of a Highland stream—the pleasures of the day always bear some proportion to the weight of the basket brought home ; and the finest scenery influences are but an indifferent compensation for an empty creel.

" By carefully studying the precepts so pithily and pleasantly enunciated here, no tyro need despair, after he has undergone his probation, of becoming a practical angler ; and even those who worthily aspire to that distinction already, and have acquired the necessary neatness of hand and quickness of eye, may have their observation not a little sharpened and their prejudices sapped. The treatise is remarkably complete in all the details of the trout-fishing art. Fresh-water trout—the causes of their decrease, the season when they are in highest condition, and every phase of their natural history—claim a chapter. All the minutiæ of an angler's equipment are gone into with quite a Gerard-Dow minuteness, and so on to artificial fly-fishing, flies, fly-dressing, May-fly fishing, and trouting with the fly. Angling with the worm, which he considers to possess one very solid advantage over fly in the superior size of the trout caught, is also copiously handled, as well as minnow and parr-tail baits. Loch-fishing, in which the accomplished angler and the tyro are most upon a par, has, nevertheless no small charm in his eyes; and his book is appropriately concluded by some precepts on 'the best means of filling a basket in May, June, July, August, and September.' The author has shown, to quote the late Mr Barnes, 'lots of grapple' in dealing with his subject; and we trust that his readers may be able to act up to the spirit of the phrase, and remember his advice when they feel the thrilling nibble, and have to go gallantly into action at a moment's notice with a Highland *Salmo ferox* in the approaching summer."

BELL'S LIFE IN LONDON.

" Without hesitation we pronounce this little treatise the best we have ever read on angling for trout with the artificial fly, worm, minnow, and other baits. It is written with most minute care by an angler of fifteen years' constant practice, of great and varied observation, unprejudiced by egotistical theory, of sound judgment, and whose wholesome knowledge of the habits of trout renders all that he says about the best modes of capturing entitled to the utmost confidence. . . . . Every young fly-fisher, desirous of becoming proficient in by far the pleasantest and best branch of the angling art, should study the excellent and manifold maxims laid down in this most valuable little treatise. The tyro that does may rest assured that he is in his right path, following a practical, experienced, clever, and conscientious guide."

NOTES AND QUERIES.

" The followers of good patient Izaak, or rather of his scholar Charles Cotton, will do well to look to a little volume just published, under the title of *The Practical Angler, or The Art of Trout-Fishing, more particularly applied to Clear Water*, by W. C. Stewart. The writer, who appears to have written his works, after the fashion of Dr. Kitchener, with the rod in one hand and the pen in the other, broaches some new theories, calculated to startle the prejudices of the brothers of the angle But he reasons well ; and as the May-fly will now be upon the waters, we advise them to give Mr Stewart's directions a fair trial. If they do, we hope they will find his promise of a well-filled pannier realised to the full."

SCOTSMAN.

"This book is the probable inauguration of a new era in the art of angling. . . . . Although the angler's library is already a pretty full one, each half-century for the last three hundred years having produced one or more pleasant and useful additions to it, we have no hesitation in saying that it cannot be complete without this little volume. Nowhere that we know of in the same compass, or indeed in any compass, is there so much valuable practical instruction to the trout-fisher. Mr. Stewart indulges but little in those graces of composition through which some of our least useful angling-books are rendered the most charming to the reader, but crams every page with information which, from its obvious accordance with common sense and sound theory, not less than from its being vouched for by an angler of large experience, and of a skill that has never yet been matched, commends itself as valuable even to the most sceptical and self-satisfied adept."

SATURDAY REVIEW.

"Mr. Stewart's book, *The Practical Angler,* entirely fulfils its title. The author, who is said to be the best fisherman in Scotland, has an object, and keeps it steadily in view—it is to teach the art of killing trout in clear water. He says, and with entire truth, that anybody can kill fish in a coloured stream. His cardinal point of faith is to fish up-stream. Here is true wisdom. A trout lies up-stream—his work is to take flies and food floating down-stream. In fishing up-stream you are behind your fish, and, great as are the capacities of a fish's eyes, it stands to reason that the angler at his tail has more chance of being undiscovered than if he charges his enemy *en face.* Next comes the advantage that in striking a fish your chances are greater in striking against him than in snatching from him. And when you have struck a fish you pull him into water that you have already fished over—you pull him down stream, leaving all the water above you undisturbed. What is meant by fly-fishing ? Of course the object is to deceive the trout into the belief that he sees a real live fly. Which is most likely to deceive him—a fly cast above him and gently floating down to him, or one cast in the ordinary fashion, and madly crossing the stream at eccentric angles and with galvanised jerks ? Real insects never cross a stream driving up against the current by superhuman, not to say superinsectine, leaps and plunges. Fish may be caught by flies drawn up and across the stream ; but nature's way is the best, and that floats flies down stream. Of course in dark and coloured waters the difference is less important ; but Mr Stewart's lesson is how to kill trout in clear water. And we heartily subscribe to his canons—with the modification that casting up stream is not to be always straight up, but diagonally, going over the whole water, but still casting upwards. Another very sensible observation of Mr. Stewart is that the colour of a fly is not half so important as the way in which it is made to fall and float on the water. A small fly and clear gut are *sine quibus non ;* and the thing to aim at is the appearance of life, not colour, in your artificial bait. A more practical, sound, sensible, and unpretending book we never read, and we recommend it without abatement or qualification."

THE FIELD.

" The modest unpretending little volume before us is decidedly welcome. *The Practical Angler*—we like the title. We are prepared to find something practical in it, and thanks be, for once we are not deceived. It is practical in every sense of the word. . . . We can recommend this little book to tyros or anglers in the transition state of every grade and shade, and even the finished practitioner may find in it something worthy of notice."

JOHN BULL.

. . . . " But the author needs no excuse, and has limited himself to no specialty. He has given us the very best handbook of angling that we know of ; and it is a material part of its merits that it occupies so small a compass ; for most anglers, however they may affect a voluminous fishing-book, are disposed to cavil at prolixity in a treatise on this science. Short as it is, the work contains all that is needed, either for the fly at the one end of the machinery, or the angler at the other. How to make your fly, how to throw it ; how to hook your fish, how to land it ; all about your own habits and those of the trout, is told in a simple and sportsmanlike style. Mr. Stewart is the Colonel Hawker of fishing."

DURHAM COUNTY ADVERTISER.

" A piscatorial friend, who ought to know something of such matters, assures us that, compared with the present volume, all previous works on the gentle craft are 'mere trash'—good old patient Izaak included   This is certainly high praise, but not more, we believe, than the work really deserves.   It professes to be a plain, practical guide (without poetry), not to the mere tyro in the art of fishing, but also to those who fondly imagine they are far beyond the rudiments of the craft.   The guide, as we have said, professes to be practical, and such it is in every sense of the word ; for although several new theories are broached, calculated to stagger old stagers, the author shows how they can all be reduced to practice with the most successful results.   In these days of book-making it is refreshing to find so much sound sense and useful information in so small a compass.   If those who strictly follow Mr. Stewart's advice do not return from streams in which trout are to be found, with well-filled creels, the sooner they resign the pursuit the better—as we feel confident nature never designed them for anglers."

NEWCASTLE JOURNAL.

" In the present little volume, which has reached a second edition, Mr. Stewart, albeit that he boasts no literary fame, has produced a work no less interesting to the general reader than highly instructive to the lover of the gentle art ; and which, by well-informed critics, has been designated as the best work yet published on the subject.   Glancing over its contents, we feel disposed to concur in this favourable verdict."

CHAMBERS'S JOURNAL.

" We would take the opportunity of remarking, that when our friends have carefully perused *The Practical Angler*, and after that, whether they take the train to the north or to the south, it will be their own fault if they do not know how to fill their basket."

ABERDEEN HERALD.

" We have never seen in so small space so many sound practical precepts upon angling, as may be found in this unpretending volume.   Every honest fisher will give this little book a hearty welcome ; he will not long remain without it."

GREENOCK TELEGRAPH.

" Mr. Stewart's work, as a whole, will, like a Murray's Guide-book to Roads and Towns, serve as a guide to rivers and streams, and will open up new views of the science of using the rod to tyros in search of trout and amusement, and to older practi-tioners, bent solely on the filling of their creels.   To one and all we commend the book ; not to piscators only, for general readers will also find in it sufficiently attractive matter to repay perusal."

DUNDEE ADVERTISER.

" The *Practical Angler* will, we confidently predict, attract the attention of the entire community of anglers, and not a few old hands will give a trial to its recommendations.   The appear-ance of the book just at the time when every sportsman is look-ing to his rod and his tackle is very seasonable, and we have no doubt it will run through several editions."

EDINBURGH EVENING COURANT.

" The book is exceedingly interesting, and should be read by every one who feels any concern in a branch of amusement and recreation in which nine-tenths of civilised mankind take delight. It is composed in a very lucid and clear style, such as the veriest tyro cannot fail to understand almost intuitively.   This is by far the most complete and practical work which has yet appeared on the subject, and there is little probability of its being super-seded by any other treatise of the kind.   We shall be surprised if the sale is not as unrivalled as its own excellence."

KELSO MAIL.

"We have derived great pleasure, and not a little information, from the perusal of this little work ; and we have no hesitation in asserting that, while to the young fisher its contents will be invaluable, even the oldest and most experienced will feel pleasure and profit in perusing its contents.   It should, and we doubt not will soon, be on the most prominent shelf of every angler's library."

BORDER ADVERTISER.

" Mr. Stewart deserves the thanks of the brotherhood gene-rally ; and the only fear we entertain regarding his production is, that if his directions are followed with the same success in every case as his own—notwithstanding what we have averred above—there *is* a likelihood of a time coming when the streams of the South will become depopulated—so great will be the havoc among the finny tribe."

AYRSHIRE EXPRESS.

"To the tyro in the art it will be an invaluable acquisition ; and even those who look upon themselves as far above par, will find many valuable hints that may, on their first piscatory excursion, help them to procure a basketful of good trout."

Printed by R. CLARK, *Edinburgh.*

www.ingramcontent.com/pod-product-compliance
Lightning Source LLC
Chambersburg PA
CBHW020115030726
47498CB00006B/2120